PEOPLE ARE THE PLAN

A LEADERSHIP APPROACH TO WINNING WITH PEOPLE

DOUG STRICKEL

ISBN 979-8-88616-863-1 (paperback)
ISBN 979-8-88616-864-8 (digital)

Christian Faith Publishing
832 Park Avenue
Meadville, PA 16335
www.christianfaithpublishing.com

Printed in the United States of America

CONTENTS

PREFACE

It was 1991, and we had moved to South Arkansas for me to begin working with a large industrial manufacturing company. We had spent the prior four years in South Louisiana, while I worked for a large national CPA firm. The CPA firm provided me outstanding exposure to various industries, developed me in several key areas, and provided me a technical background for business that has proven very helpful over the years. That firm also opened my eyes to the people side of things in business. While the technical developmental opportunities at the CPA firm were outstanding, the firm's environment was one of extreme internal competition with very little focus on leadership development or supervisory skills. The overriding atmosphere was very self-focused as the firm's goal for the employees was to either perform well and advance or find employment elsewhere. Many employees did find employment with clients, which oftentimes was a mutual benefit to the company and to the employee leaving.

The office environment was competitive to say the least. I was very surprised at the lack of outward value for people displayed by such a large percentage of the management team in the office. While the technical skills were emphasized, the interpersonal aspects of leading others were essentially ignored. Now don't get me wrong, there were exceptions to this depiction, but overall, that was the predominant atmosphere and focus at that time in this particular office.

I really thought the change to a large manufacturing company would provide more of a team concept and allow me to focus on contributing to the success of one business as opposed to changing clients every few weeks as I did with the firm. While I quickly began to enjoy working with the local management team, there were quite a few opportunities to get engaged, to help promote a more people-focused workplace, and to use that platform as the engine to drive improved operational results. I was thankful for the opportunity and looked forward to the change as my wife and I were quickly settling into the small town life.

This regained focus on people being the engine to drive improvement took on an entirely different meaning though within my first six months of work at the facility. The event that triggered this additional focus for me was a visit from the CEO and several members of his staff. They were coming to our facility site to review the operational results with the management teams and to take a tour of both facilities. There were two facilities on the same site, and they operated very closely with one another at that time. The larger facility was a primary mill manufacturing large rolls of paper used by other manufacturers to produce various types of paper bags. The smaller operation was actually a bag plant that took the large rolls of paper and produced various type of paper bags for cement companies, pet food companies, food companies, and other companies that required packaging for their products. I was initially assigned to the bag plant and was chosen to present our financial results during the meeting. I was also chosen to lead one of the tour groups through the facility during the visit.

On the day of the visit, we were instructed to wear business formal dress to work that day to match the appearance of our guests. There were no casual days in the corporate office or by corporate staff members back then. So I put on the old CPA suit with my steel-toed boots and went to work that day. It was quite a sight that day in both of the facilities with managers wearing formal business attire in a very dirty, hot environment, but that's what we had to do back then.

From what I can recall so many years later, the presentations and tour went fine, but it was a discussion near the end of the tour that impacted me the most. Toward the end of the tour, we were standing on a mezzanine platform looking out over the facility when the number two guy in the company looked at me and asked a very pointed question. He asked, "Doug, what do you see out there?"

I paused for a moment not knowing where he was going with that question and just replied, "I see people working and just doing their jobs."

He quickly corrected me by saying, "Those people are all liabilities. You need to figure out how to get by with fewer of them!"

Now that comment was not necessarily representative of the company at that time, nor is it necessarily representative of the company today, but it was a very impactful comment in the moment. Here I was, six months with the company and in my midtwenties. I had a heart for people and really wanted to make an impact helping the business to be successful, but also creating a better workplace for everyone there. I don't remember much about the rest of that day, but I have never forgotten that encounter. Not only did I strongly disagree with that assessment of people being no more than liabilities; but rather I made a commitment that day that I would do everything I could to value people, to improve the work environment for people, and to develop sound business strategies that could be executed well and not always be based on fewer people.

So some thirty-plus years later, I want to share with you a plan on how to accomplish that type of a goal. I want to share a plan on how to really value people in the workplace and allow that focus to be a key driver in achieving desired business results. This plan bridges solid strategy with a people focused approach regardless of the business or mission of the organization. I can't say that business shouldn't always be cost conscious and not overstaff for prolonged periods of time, but I want to emphasize the value of the worker and elevate their status beyond just another cost input (or liability in the case of my encounter with senior leadership). I hope that you find the ideas shared in this book helpful to you in several ways. Furthermore, I hope these ideas provide you an effective basis to drive the results you need; but I also hope they help you strengthen, and in some cases regain, your focus on valuing people. I have made a commitment to help develop leaders that will change the workplace to make it one that is a desirable place to work. With the changing workforce that we see today and the desire of so many to find meaningful work with a healthy work-life balance, I can't think of a better time to share this concept.

The concept is really pretty straightforward. We need to change the mentality in our workplace from one of a renter to an owner. Now when I say renter in this context, I am not directing a negative connotation to renting by any means. We have all rented at one time or another, and there is nothing wrong or negative about that at all. Rather, I am talking about the negative impact of taking that renter mentality to the workplace and comparing that view to the overriding benefits of having an owner mentality within the workforce.

In the chapters that follow, I will share key concepts to changing the culture to one of owners and discuss the benefits of that change. It takes work to change a culture, and it takes leaders doing the work to make that change. It all starts with leadership. I want to help you be that leader and ultimately be a leader worthy of following.

INTRODUCTION

Businesses of all types are facing staffing challenges that many of us have never experienced nor anticipated. Whether it's the "Great Resignation," the fallout from the pandemic, or just a change in the mindset of the younger generations, there is no doubt that businesses are facing increased challenges in staffing. These staffing challenges must be dealt with to ensure businesses continue to operate effectively and that supply chain needs are met. We have all witnessed the result of supply chain breakdowns and the effects on communities across the country. Lives are impacted when business is not functioning as designed, and we need to address these issues.

The answer to this problem is more based on a culture change than a new business strategy. What we need is a different view of the workplace and not a new governmental incentive, a new strategic plan, nor a new compensation approach. This new view of the workplace is one where we move our employees working for the company to team members that take on an ownership mentality in the organization. For years, workers have operated with a renter mentality in the workplace. Supervisors and managers at all levels have oftentimes driven this renter mentality. We tell people what we need them to do and hold them accountable for getting the work done. Supervisors and managers get work done through others because that's their job, and that function will always be a key role for these positions. Directing others can be done differently though as we look to change the way we get work done through others.

What I am proposing is a culture change where these same supervisors and managers go beyond their historic roles and become leaders, leaders that influence change in the workplace to transform a renter mentality to one of an owner view in the workplace. What

I am suggesting is a culture change where our team members view themselves differently, contribute at a different level, and become engaged at a much deeper level. We have talked about engagement in the workplace for years now, and I am proposing an approach to take engagement to a level that resolves staffing issues and drives performance improvement in all areas.

While these issues are more pressing today than thirty years ago, the challenges of leading people well and developing a desirable place for people to work have been a focus area for me for my entire working career. In the chapters that follow, I will share my basis for this approach using "my story" examples along with specific actions that I used in leading people through the various aspects of this transformation. The examples are very practical steps that can be taken to develop this same ownership culture in your organization. The specific steps are a summary of what I have implemented in a manufacturing environment for the very purpose of creating a better workplace and using that foundation to generate improved operating and financial results. The "I's" describing the attributes of an owner that are noted in those ownership chapters are proven concepts with very tactical steps and ideas on how to implement each of them. While the ideas shared are conceptual in nature, you will find very specific suggestions to act on for each of the concepts to be very tactical and applicable for any organization.

Make no mistake, this approach is a leadership-based model to generate change in the culture of the workplace. This book is not a management book on how to develop strategy or refine your business plans. Those strategic businesses concepts are important aspects of business, but my focus here is to help you lead more effectively by equipping you with new ideas on building engagement and transforming your work environment. Specifically, I will outline the benefits and process to change your organization's workplace culture to one of team member ownership. Changing culture will be a tough challenge and will require the leader to engage at a high level. We can change the culture, create a more desirable work environment for our people, and improve the financial results by focusing on an existing resource. That resource is our existing workforce! People are the focus of this plan.

CHAPTER 1

RENTER TO OWNER

My story

It was 2001, and I was just promoted to my first plant manager assignment. The facility was in Northeast Arkansas, and while I knew very little about the business nor the facility, it was an opportunity for me to be the leader of a business employing approximately 150 people. As the general manager, I would be responsible for everything operationally, commercially, and environmentally that was associated with the facility. I had no experience in this particular container business, but I did have a solid background in operational systems and overall business strategy from my prior job assignments. I also had the opportunity to participate in the engagement process at my former facility and would be bringing plenty of life experiences to this new role.

What I saw within the first few weeks of work in the new facility was nothing less than a complete disaster. The facility did not have solid safety systems, and there were far too many people getting hurt. The safety files of recent injuries were the most I had ever seen or heard of in a twelve-month period. The facility had no effective quality program, and there were way too many customer complaints. Some days, I saw more trucks returning with rejected products than leaving with new products on them. There was no reliability system in place, and the machine operations were just operating on what

I referred to as the hope management system. We just hoped the machines would keep running each day. I found myself hoping I could go home each night and not get a phone call regarding some machine reliability issue. Hope management is never a good plan. Needless to say, we were losing a lot of money each month, morale was terrible, and things overall were much worse than I anticipated.

I knew I had to start taking action. The facility had no operating systems in place, and the employee base was about as disengaged as one could imagine. I had spent the last ten years in an environment where we maintained solid systems in all areas of the operation and operated a solid business with fairly strong employee involvement. In this prior assignment, we had developed a comprehensive communication plan that really engaged the workforce. We were also a long-standing business and were very highly respected in the community. Now I was in a facility that had none of those attributes, and we were just one of many companies located within a large industrial complex just outside a much larger city. What a contrast!

Over the next few months, I balanced my time between developing and implementing key operational systems, making leadership changes and initiating contact with our key customers that we had let down on far too many occasions with poor quality and unreliable service. I referred to these customer visits as my "Apology and Recommitment Tour." I planned on being direct with the customers by accepting prior faults and directing them to what we would be doing to provide a better experience for them in the future. The discussions would be tough, but acknowledging the poor quality and service up front should be helpful. There was no need to argue about it. We had been a poor supplier. Once we all agreed on that fact, we could move forward with how we were going to improve.

Getting to know plant personnel was another major initiative to focus on during those first few weeks and months. Working with plant personnel to develop key systems was an outstanding way for me to learn the business and get to know people. This time period was prior to corporate-driven systems and processes that are now in place and standardized across the company. Back then, local leaders had a great deal of influence and autonomy, but they were also on their own to some extent with respect to defining the operating and commercial processes to be followed in their organization. We were able to work together to develop and implement these key operating systems in a fairly short period of time. The people were a great help to me in this process, and I could have never developed these systems without their support.

It was a tough challenge organizing the leadership team to ensure the right folks were in the right places, but it had to be done. Regardless of the operation's size or purpose, there must be alignment within the leadership team if that team is going to succeed. Within any team are individuals with different experiences, backgrounds, and character. I prefer loyalty and commitment over experience and knowledge any day. While, like most of you, I would prefer to have all of these attributes, but given only one, I will always choose character. I can ensure someone learns the job and gains experience, but character is hard to teach. Loyalty and commitment are key facets of character that are so instrumental when you are trying to initiate change in a new environment.

We did have to make several important personnel moves to get the right folks in the right places. A leadership team has to be on the same page, or it won't matter how much they individually know. We gave up some experience and suffered through some uneasy days to get the right people in the right places so we could move forward as a leadership team. There were some tough conversations and some reassignments that would be necessary. Some key members of the management team chose to leave, and that was okay. We were left with fewer managers, but everyone that remained was fully committed. I am not sure they fully understood where we were going, but they were fully beside me in the effort.

Finally, the "Apology and Recommitment Tour" went well, and we maintained our customer base through the transformation process. The key message in these customer meetings was to own what we did wrong and acknowledge where we had let various customers down. There was no reason to argue or make excuses. We were there to own the past but also to project a better tomorrow with some specific focus areas that would make a difference. Regardless of what we told them, we had to back it up with solid execution as soon as we left those meetings. The keys were implementing solid planning, reliability, and quality systems in the facility. I also knew we needed engaged employees that cared, but that's not something to share with a customer when you are trying to hang on to business!

These three key steps of implementing systems, organizing the right leadership team, and solidifying the customer base were just the foundation for what was to come though. While these three initial steps made a noticeable improvement in several key areas of the plant and settled things down to a degree, they alone did not achieve what we needed for sustainable change in the facility. We had one last major focus area to tackle. This one could not be accomplished until the foundation was built by installing those systems and organizing the leadership team.

We now needed to start changing the culture of the workplace and the mindset of the workforce. Up to this point, we had some really committed workers and yet many more that were just showing up most days and doing what we asked them to do at their respective job assignments. We had a workforce that I would describe as having a renter mentality. Most of our workforce just wanted to get their eight hours in, stay under the radar, and go home each day or night. We really needed a group of people that would function as a team and take on an owner mentality. We started working on developing that type of an ownership culture. That type of change takes time and a great deal of effort by the leader and the leadership team. I would ultimately try to install this type of ownership culture as I took on expanded job assignments in the organization as well. I will discuss the steps in building that type culture in later chapters, but let me first clarify what is meant by a renter mentality as opposed to a culture with an owner mentality.

RENTER VS. OWNER

As I previously mentioned, the use of the term renter here is not intended to be a negative connotation at all, but rather I'm talking in terms of the workplace mentality. Renting and renters have a very necessary place in society. Renting is a common business transaction across the globe and has been for centuries. When we use those attributes in the work environment, however, the characteristics can lead to some frustrating results for the leader of the organization, as well as very limited engagement by the workforce.

Renter description:

1. Renters are there until something better comes along.
2. Renters seldom take responsibility when things go wrong.
3. Renters pass along problems and don't get involved in solving the issue.
4. Renters don't pay attention to details.
5. Renters are generally not looking to improve things.

Now if you take a look at those five items, I think we would all agree that we have all been there before as we rented items; and those factors are acceptable in areas such as home rentals, vacation rentals, vehicle rentals, and rentals of other tangible items. However, when you apply those attributes to workforce mentality, the outlook doesn't look quite as positive. I wonder how many of us, if we were being real honest though, would say the description above reflects that of our workforce today. We are in a time of staffing challenges and labor shortages not seen in years. We see workers changing jobs more than we have experienced in a long time. Job satisfaction appears to be a struggle with more people today than was ever expressed in prior periods. Is the description of a workforce with a renter mentality one that you deal with on a regular basis?

The impact of a renter mentality in the workforce usually requires the management team to be very involved in all aspects of the operation. While that involvement is not a bad thing necessarily, it does place a lot of pressure on the supervisors and managers. With that type of environment, a few people are making all the decisions and bearing all the load for the successful operation of the organization. Not only does this renter mentality put a strain on the management group on a daily basis, it also places a ceiling on just how successful the operation can be in achieving results. With this workplace mentality, the success all rides on the talent of a few people telling everyone else what to do and how to do it. Take away one of those key people for any length of time, and the operation may suffer greatly and will surely not be sustainable at a desired level of results. The ceiling on success is based on the talent and impact of a few key people.

Many of us have struggled through work environments, such as the one I have described above with the renter mentality. We have worked in those type environments and likely even managed through those type operations at one time or another. Needless to say, I think I have described most of the work environments in our country to some degree. I'm describing an environment where so many just want to punch in, do what's expected to stay out of trouble, and punch out. I had an employee tell me early on in my career that he just wanted to do his time and go home. It sounded almost like he was dealing with a prison sentence. Another told me one time to just tell him what I wanted. He wasn't paid to think, but rather he was just paid to do. How sad are those comments?

Couple those concerns with the increasing focus on work-life balance, and I think we see that the workplace has become something far too many dread going to each day. Don't get me wrong, I am all for balancing time at work and at home, but I hate that we have to view work as the necessary evil. Yes, it is hard at times and not nearly as much fun as hanging out at the lake, but it can be a rewarding and meaningful part of our lives. Work doesn't have to be something to dread. I really hope we can make the workplace an extension of our life and not just something we have to plow through to get to something more desirable.

Let's take a look at a different cultural focus, one of an ownership mentality:

Owner mentality:

1. Owners take full responsibility for everything.
2. Owners pay attention to details.
3. Owners seek to resolve problems quickly.
4. Owners seek to improve things.

5. Owners care for each other, care for the business, and are engaged in all things.

I think we would all love to have a workforce that had those attributes noted above. The attributes above are a huge contrast from those of the renter mentality previously described. These people are not just punching in, doing their eight, and staying off the radar. These people are fully invested! When you start to think of the benefits of having a workforce with this mindset, you can see that the benefits are numerous and obvious. This culture doesn't just happen, but rather it takes commitment and work by the leader and leadership team to achieve this type of environment in the workplace.

This type of workforce thinking can impact results in all areas of the operation. When people become owners and take responsibility for everything in their sphere of influence, managers and supervisors can focus on improvements, strategic issues, and removing obstacles and not get sidetracked dealing with the basic "issues of the day." When people pay attention to details and look to resolve problems rather than ignoring items and just passing along problems, more issues get resolved, and the issues get resolved timely. When everyone is engaged and looking to drive improvement, there is a culture that brings out the best in everyone and leads to a high degree of mutual accountability. The results exceed what could have been accomplished with just a supervisor pushing the group along.

An ownership mentality also leads to increased employee retention. With the staffing issues facing so many companies today, who wouldn't benefit from retention improvements? Employee turnover and staffing shortages are costing companies far too much these days. We can try a lot of different techniques to retain our people, but the one I have found most useful over time is this concept of ownership. Sure, we have to maintain competitive pay and benefits, but that ownership mentality can set us apart from others in the marketplace. Retention is not only positive in and of itself, but strong retention also benefits the hiring process when staffing additions are needed. You have a culture that creates a work environment that people desire to be a part of and want to join the organization. Trust me, word gets out if you have a workplace culture that is desirable! If people need to work, why shouldn't they choose to seek employment with you?

If you have ever experienced a workplace culture like the ownership one described here, you can testify about the impact it can have on all aspects of an operation. Over time, the safety results reflect it, the operational results will reflect it, the commercial results reflect it, and most importantly, the mission of the organization is achieved with less burden on any single individual. The other benefit is that the process allows for results to be sustainable.

This idea of culture change to one of ownership is a concept that is often overlooked. We talk so much about strategy, and I will agree that strategy for any organization is important. However, don't place too much emphasis on strategy. Strategy without execution leads to failure. That's right, the most impressive strategy ever designed is a failure if it can't be executed well. Many companies invest thousands of dollars on strategy development, create managerial positions focused on strategy, and pay consultants to guide strategy discussions, but they often ignore culture development in their organization.

Strategy can be described as asking the question: Are we doing right things? Execution can be described as asking the question: Are we doing things right? Those two questions contain the same exact words in a different order. Both have to be answered yes to be successful. Culture is often the key to sustained execution. A culture of ownership and an understanding of capability can be coupled with a solid (doesn't have to be great) strategy to lead to success. Culture will drive that execution. An ownership culture may be just the piece that is needed in many operations today.

The rest of the story

So after developing those operating systems, getting the right management team in place, and investing in the customer relationships (remember the Apology and Recommitment Tour), we began the process of culture change in the facility. We had a workforce of people that were largely renters, and we needed to lead them to being one of owners. Culture is defined as the collective beliefs and actions of a group of people over time, and we were tasked with changing a long-standing view of the workplace to promote different actions. We had to present a vision of a better way and one that benefited everyone involved. We had to not only talk about what had to change but really explain why it mattered to the worker. The old adage of "What's in it for me?" was a conscious thought that we had to clarify at each step of this culture change. It was hard, tedious work, but it did pay off. It took almost eighteen months to fully realize the change and completely see the new ownership culture in action, but it was well worth the effort. Sure, we tried some things and adjusted along the way. There were some mistakes made (I have sure made my share), but we never got off course. The vision was a culture of owners that would create a desirable workplace and one that would improve results. We achieved both and would continue to build on this effort for the remaining time we had together. There were always opportunities to improve and further develop this type of approach. In the end, we had one of the most engaging workforces that I have ever seen. We had owners throughout the facility on every shift and in every aspect of the operation. We realized improvement in safety, operational metrics, commercial results, and financial performance. More importantly to me, we cared for and valued our people, who in turn, cared for one another. Our workforce was highly engaged, and we created something special for them. Many of the leaders would advance and carry this approach with them to other job opportunities as they promoted within the company to build similar cultures. If I had to sum it up, the key words were *valuing people, mutual accountability,* and *shared responsibility.*

Key learnings:

1. Renter mentality in the workforce is common and limits what can be accomplished.
2. With staffing issues today, a move to an ownership culture may be the answer needed.
3. An ownership culture provides some very clear benefits to any organization.

4. Strategy, execution, and culture all work together to yield success.
5. Culture is the sustaining factor in any organization.

CHAPTER 2

MORE THAN HIGH PERFORMANCE WORK SYSTEMS

My story

It was the mid-1990s, and I had been assigned to the bag converting plant for several years. I did have regular interaction with the mill side of the business, so I was gaining exposure across the entire complex. Both operations were union represented, and things were pretty stable in both operations for the most part. The facility was the largest employer in the city and county which commanded a lot of respect and awareness in the community. The facility was started back in the late 1920s and had been the employer of choice for generations of families in the area. Managers would come and go over the years, but the bulk of the workforce was homegrown and home supported.

Pay rates, stability, and good benefits were really what attracted folks to the facility. The operations were essentially 24/7, 365 days a year. The plant would shut down more often than the mill, which was only down for the much publicized one-week annual shutdown. While the jobs were stable and there was no real issue attracting people to apply, working at the facilities was hard work that involved rotating shifts that never stopped for the most part. If you asked employees if they enjoyed their job, you would get a mixed response depending on who you asked the question. There always did seem to be some level of division between management and labor as people termed it at the mill. I never quite understood the division or bought into it. The hard hat colors were different. The parking areas were different, and it just seemed like some antiquated practices were still in place that drove a slight wedge between supervisory folks and the hourly paid workforce.

I tried very hard to fight the divisiveness every chance that was afforded to me. In that small town, we went to church with all types of folks that worked at the facility, either the mill or the plant. I coached every little league sport offered in town and had kids from both salaried families and hourly paid families on those teams. We even lived in an area of town where both types of families were living. Maybe being somewhat new, it was easier for me to not get caught up in the imaginary walls of how people were compensated. Not to mention, I made a point to get to know as many people as possible in the facility, regardless of their position. When you actually take the time to get to know someone, things just change in a work relationship. In addition, there was so much knowledge in the folks closest to where the jobs were being done that I sought out opportunities to ask questions and let people talk about what they did every day. After all, these folks were the experts regarding their respective subject matters, and most people like to talk about what they know and what they do.

I assume my focus in the people area of our work and my regular leadership discussions with my managerial counterparts led me to receive one of the company's first invites to a training session on how to move work teams to a high performance work system (HPWS). In the mid-1990s, HPWSs were a very popular topic of discussion. Several companies had shared about their success moving toward an HPWS that was focused on departmental goal setting, decentralized decision-making, increased information sharing, and oftentimes an incentive-based reward system. While an HPWS could look very different from one place to another depending on the elements implemented, these systems were all based on decentralization of control with the intent to generate better business results. There was clear evidence that some companies that had moved toward an HPWS were having success. The consultants had no doubt convinced our company's leadership team to explore the possibility of moving toward such a work environment.

I was assigned to attend a training session to learn the approach and ultimately to take the key learnings and messages back to the facility for further evaluation by the local management team. The session I attended was uniquely referred to as "Pasta School." It was not your typical lecture environment, but rather a hands-on demonstration of high performance work systems/teams using pasta making as our business platform. I am not naturally drawn to events that I don't know anyone and get immediately assigned to a work team, but this group did a nice job of getting us acclimated very quickly. For several days, we made various types of pasta (actually did make edible pasta) and ran the business from several rented-out hotel rooms at a conference center near the corporate office. Now we did not actually sell the products, but we did transact business with the seminar trainers as we learned how to decentralize the operation, engage everyone in the mission, and leverage the skills of the team to generate the most advantageous results. Looking back, it was a good week and one that further validated my commitment to people and the value placed on each worker. I'm not sure I retained much about pasta making, but I did strengthen my resolve to engage people and to create more desirable work environment for our people.

OWNERSHIP CULTURE AND HIGH PERFORMANCE WORK SYSTEMS NOT THE SAME

While HPWS are based heavily on implementing a new system that does in fact change the workplace culture, when I talk about creating a culture of ownership, I am referring to something very different. Most HPWS approaches are based heavily on decentralizing control and decision-making, enhancing information sharing, collaborating on goal setting, and expanding team concepts within an organization. None of those are necessarily bad things at all. In some places, those type of approaches can and have worked very well. That approach is just not what I am referring to when I talk about a culture of employee ownership.

A culture of ownership is not based on a system, although work systems do play an important part in any organization. A culture of ownership does not decentralize power and ask managers and supervisors to give up the role of key decision maker, nor does it diminish the role and impact of those responsible for the organization. In fact, a culture of ownership is heavily dependent on the manager or supervisor stepping outside that role and truly being a leader. To be honest, an organization can't move toward an ownership culture without a leader taking that step and creating an environment where those working for the organization are given the opportunity to move from employee to team member, from laborer to valued member of the team, and ultimately from a renter mentality to an owner mentality.

While an HPWS is heavily focused on how the process is directed, a culture of ownership is more focused on valuing the people in the organization. An ownership culture is one that sees value in the individual in their entirety. We value not only what an individual can do but also what they think, what they question, and what they can add to the organization beyond a pure job description. In fact, in a true ownership culture, people are not limited to the confinements of a job description. Sure, everyone has a function that is clearly defined; but as an owner, the interest levels and input can carry over into various aspects of the organization as anyone with an owner mentality would naturally possess. An ownership culture is not limited by the typical organizational chart. Sure, everyone knows who they report to in the structure, but that relationship enhances one's performance and does not limit that performance.

While an HPWS can be somewhat threatening to those in charge as decision-making is oftentimes decentralized, an ownership culture compliments command and control as opposed to replacing it. The manager is not giving up anything, but rather gaining a team of associates that are fully engaged in the mission and hopefully the purpose of the organization. The more a leader can connect people to the mission and ultimately the purpose of the organization, the better chance the culture will be one of ownership. Ownership culture is not a power struggle but rather a responsibility-sharing approach and only happens when the leader values people and places them at the center of the leader's purpose in leading.

In the chapters that follow, I will provide details of how one can implement this change in culture and move toward one of engaging people to a level that they not only feel like owners but act like owners. The following chapters will take the basic concept of employee engagement and provide specific actions that can actually change the culture in a manner that creates a sustainable approach to the workplace. This concept will address current staffing issues, a changing workforce that wants more than a paycheck, and the challenges managers face today in achieving business results. You will see more than just a theory to be tried, but rather a specific plan to be implemented to finally achieve a culture change in the workplace that takes employee engagement to a much higher level. This concept is not a fad, but rather a sustainable way to execute your business plan, drive your key systems, and achieve the results you need with a workforce that serves as the driving engine to your success.

THE REST OF THE STORY

HPWS were subsequently trialed at a few facilities but never really took off within our company. While some others' companies had success, many others decided, for various reasons, to not go down that road. I think the level of change and the decentralization of control was just too much for some key executives within our company to get comfortable with at that time. It would have been a big change and could have easily been disruptive to many facilities if not implemented very carefully. I really think there were some large gaps in overall engagement in far too many places to effectively move to an HPWS in an efficient and effective manner. In fact, decentralization of control may have just been a nonstarter for too many influential leaders. While we never really moved forward with this approach, it did help to further refine my personal thoughts of what the workplace should be like for everyone involved. It was a good example for me of seeking to learn and find key learnings from every experience to help shape, refine, and ultimately lead to a new idea or concept that can ultimately benefit others. Don't get me wrong, there is some level of overlap in HPWS and this concept of ownership culture, and some organizations will succeed with either one or a combination of the two concepts. My focus will be on valuing people and creating an atmosphere for culture change that I have discussed. Also, please don't regard my comments on valuing people as some passive approach to leadership. This culture change that I describe is based on not only this valuing concept but also on one of mutual accountability. Owners are accountable and held to a higher standard. There is nothing soft or passive about that approach. To really value the entire team, we must hold everyone accountable. Engagement, care, value, and accountability must all mutually exist for an ownership culture to be achieved and sustained.

Key learnings:

1. Ownership culture is people focused first and not system focused as the priority.
2. Ownership culture is based on valuing people for more than just what they do.
3. Ownership culture is not about giving up power, but rather sharing the accountability and responsibility.
4. HPWS and ownership culture do have areas overlap and can coexist, but there are differences too that enable them to stand alone distinctly as well.

CHAPTER 3

THE LEADERS' ROLE IN ESTABLISHING CULTURE

My story

I t was one thing to work on establishing a culture of ownership in a single facility but quite another to start introducing these concepts to multiple facilities. After being with the company for approximately twenty years, I was given the assignment as a regional general manager over eleven different operating facilities in the southern part of the United States. Each of these facilities was both similar and yet unique at the same time. They were similar in the sense that they were all in the same business producing various forms of paper-based packaging products. However, each one of these facilities, having a unique workforce, management team, and experience base, presented a different set of challenges. Each facility had a unique culture as well that was largely influenced by either a long-standing facility leader or the community influence that provided the bulk of the workforce. In either case, there was always some form of culture in place.

My first step to address culture change was always to assess where the facility was currently with respect to their engagement level and management style of the managerial team. We had to know where we were starting from before we could lay out a plan for moving forward. What I saw over the years was quite an array of engagement levels, managerial styles, workforce experience, and plant cultures. Every plant had a culture of some sort, but some were not necessarily what I desired as a regional manager. With that said, I did see some outstanding models of engagement and leadership during my initial attempt to drive this cultural change to one of ownership mentality while working with these facilities and serving them as their regional general manager.

As a basic next step in any plant, I had to ensure the local manager and management team felt like owners. There was no way I could be successful in leading them to develop a culture of ownership in their facility if they didn't personally feel like they were "owners." We took this first step in each of the facilities by first allowing each facility leader to develop his/her own annual objectives for the year. I provided some overall regional objectives, gave them some metric-based goals, and allowed them to use those items as a guideline to develop their specific facility objectives. While we met to discuss these objectives and made some adjustments to ensure we were aligned on a successful strategy, the facility leaders had a great deal of input into this process.

Following that process, which took no more than a week to accomplish, we then proceeded to talk through a general business plan based on their facility's capability, strengths, and market opportunities. Here again, the facility leaders had a great deal of input into the development of the plan with the full knowledge that they would need to execute this plan to achieve their objectives. The plan and preceding objectives would then be shared with supervisory personnel that could in turn develop their respective objectives to support the overall facility. The goal was to create ownership and a feeling of autonomy while still supporting the overriding needs of the regional business plan and ultimately the company as a whole.

From there, we established a basic decision-making protocol that provided the local leaders with as much authority as possible while I was still available for discussion, counseling, guidance, and support in any number of ways. We agreed on parameters for this approach and moved forward immediately with a focus on mutual trust and regular communication. My goal was to ensure these managers were empowered to "own it." I was available to guide, support, and offer consulting-type input when needed; but they would lead their respective facilities. Yes, I did have to intervene from time to time and be the manager when things got off track, but that was not a regular occurrence. And the intervention did not undermine the focus or detract from our organizational objective.

Once the foundation was in place at the manager level at each facility, I could then begin to create an ownership focus at the supervisory level. The key here was to get each supervisor thinking and acting as if they were the owner/CEO of the area they were responsible for leading. This step was a little more challenging because I was not only trying to influence a significant number of supervisors across eleven facilities; but these individuals had various backgrounds, skill levels, and views on supervising. In addition, while the facility leaders all enjoyed the autonomy and ownership at the overall plant level, it would be a little different for some of them to allow others to own different aspects of the facility that the manager had been so invested in over the years.

Needless to say, some facilities moved along faster than others at this stage. I would spend time on facility visits meeting with supervisors on each of the shifts. Usually those visits required two or more meetings at each facility due to the three-shift operations. While those discussions were tiring for me, they gave me a chance to interact directly with those leading on the front line and share my vision for a culture of ownership in the workplace. Those meetings were priceless! I had a chance to interact with some outstanding individuals in facilities all over a five-state area. I'll admit not everyone bought into the idea wholeheartedly, but the concept had some level of appeal to just about everyone. If I was going to be successful rolling this plan out, these folks would be the key. Nothing would change with respect to culture if the concept was not embraced at the level closest to those leading the workforce on a daily basis. In fact, any engagement focus must be embraced by frontline leaders for it to be successful. Those leading on the front line are the key to engagement and any type of culture change regardless of the facility, the business, or the structure. Frontline buy-in was now the key, and no longer was I the central focus to the plan. I was just there to share the vision, equip the leaders, and remove obstacles.

THE THREE C'S TO A LEADERS' SUCCESS IN ESTABLISHING CULTURE

Credibility

Regardless of what aspect of leadership we are talking about, the first essential attribute for any leader is credibility. Without credibility, there will be no effective leadership. People will not follow someone that is not credible. I often speak to groups and ask them to share the most important attribute of any leader. I hear great responses every time I ask that question. I hear people respond with words such as *trustworthy, honest, knowledgeable, visionary, self-sacrificing,* and many other really great qualities of a good leader. I seldom ever hear the word *credibility* shared though. While all those aforementioned attributes are great, they all lead to one being a credible leader. So when I say credibility is the first key to being a successful leader, I am really just rolling all those wonderful qualities up into one word that embraces all of them and provides the basis for why it matters.

Credibility is the foundation for leadership. Similar to building a house where the foundation has to be in place first, has to be solid, and may not get a lot of attention later on, credibility serves that same purpose with leadership. It's not the outward appealing part of leadership, but without credibility, nothing else will matter. It may go unnoticed, but if there is ever a "crack" in it, the rest of one's leadership impact will suffer and could actually crumble. Credibility may take on various attacks from the outside environment from time to time, but if the foundation is strong, the leadership impact has even more influence.

One doesn't walk into a managerial or supervisory role and have instant credibility as a leader. Building credibility is like building that foundation on a house. It takes time to be done correctly, but over time, it gains strength as it "settles." Whether you have been with your team for an extended period and need to work on building or regaining credibility to be a more effective leader or whether you are new to the team and want to establish yourself as a leader, the following ideas will help you in this endeavor of building credibility.

1. Ensure you are technically competent. You don't have to be an expert in every facet of the operation or necessarily know more than more than everyone else, but you need to have enough knowledge to gain the respect and trust of those people that you want to lead and to follow you. Work at your trade to get this knowledge and be able to talk intelligently on any subject related to your team's assignment. Spend time getting an understanding of the operation. Go visit other sites and spend time with counterparts that have more knowledge and experience than you possess. Read, study, and do whatever you need to become technically competent. Again, you don't have to be the expert, but you need to put the time in to be knowledgeable.

2. Lead by example. Your actions will speak louder than your words. Your words are important! Nothing kills credibility faster than a prospective leader that doesn't lead by example. Don't ask others to do anything you don't expect of yourself. Hold yourself to a higher standard. Remember there are no off-camera moments for a leader (both at work and off work)! When building credibility with your team, everything you say and do matters. Pay particular attention to how you lead in stressful situations. These situations are character-revealing moments and can really define a leader. People are watching, so be prepared before the moment arrives.

3. Communicate honestly and timely with responses to your people. Don't tell people what they want to hear, but rather tell them what they need to hear. Your people need the truth no matter how uncomfortable it may be for you. Your team may not like the message, but they will respect and trust the messenger. If you have the people's long-term best interest in mind, that basis for your decision-making and ultimate messaging will serve you well. Keep your commit-

ments and get back to people timely on issues. Again, they may not always like the message, but they can trust that you are looking out for their best interest and know that you will respond to them timely.

4. Share both the good and bad news; be transparent. Be open with your team about what's going well and what needs to be improved. The messaging should be balanced when possible. People need to know what's important, how they are doing, and how they can help. If you want people to become owners, you need to keep them informed. Don't just go to your people when you need something or want to address poor performance. Go to them with good news, praise, and positive recognition too. They need to see balance in their leader to move toward trust.

5. Practice being present. You have to spend time with people to build trust and ultimately gain credibility with them. The old term *management by walking around* (MBWA) is a perfect example of this approach. That term *MBWA* is essentially the practice of presence of the leader investing with the followers (being present). When times are tough, share the pain, and be present with the team. Don't disappear when struggles come, but increase your presence and assist where you can. Don't just spend time with people, but rather be intentional with that time and invest in these relationships! Sure, take advantage of opportunities when they come up, but also be intentional with the pursuit of these opportunities.

6. Take responsibility for bad and deflect praise for the good. Nothing builds credibility more than for a team to see their leader stand up for them and take responsibility or blame for things that go wrong. Never pass the buck to the team, but rather own it in front of them. Conversely, when things go well, give them the praise and recognition publicly whenever that opportunity arises. You can always deal with negative issue within the privacy of a team meeting, but take the blame for the bad and deflect the praise for the

good publicly. You aren't looking to protect or elevate your-self here, but rather looking to build credibility with you team. You will also build credibility with your boss at the same time. Your team's performance is your performance, so no need blaming anyone.

7. Provide consistent expectations and accountability. Don't change the expectations on people without notice or too often. Hold everyone to the same level of accountability and don't play favorites. Everyone matters, and everyone needs to do their part. Consistency with accountability is essential in building credibility with the team. You have to be careful here not to get too close to some of the team members and jeopardize your objectivity. Sure get close, but not so close you can't be consistent with expectations. Consistency is key when building credibility with the entire team!

I assure you that if you practice those seven items consistently with your team, they will see that you care about them and that you have their best interest in mind. They will understand accountability and trust their leader to guide them correctly. In the end, you will have credibility with the team and be able to lead them going forward. Ultimately, you will be able to take your team to a place that they couldn't go on their own. It's not about you being liked, but rather about you being respected and known as a credible leader.

Clarify the vision

We often think that a visionary leader is just one that comes up with a grand idea or plan and everything falls into place. Quite often, that is far from the truth. Establishing a vision of a better work environment where there is a culture of ownership is one thing, but clarifying this vision and establishing a culture is something much more difficult. Clarifying a vision for others can be hard work and take time. While it may sound like just making a proclamation in a group meeting, we all know that culture change is a lot more involved than just making an announcement to a group of people. Culture change is a time-consuming process that can take on many different aspects depending on where you are starting from with the team. I want to share just a few thoughts on how to clarify the vision and of an ownership culture with your team.

1. Communicate the vision. It sounds like a natural first step, but go further than just outlining your vision. In our case, we are talking about moving toward a culture of ownership in the workplace. In other words, moving from a renter mentality to an owner mentality in our workplace is the overriding objective. From there, we have to convey a picture of a better tomorrow if we follow this path of change. We have to connect with why it should matter to everyone hearing the message and why it should be important to them. We need to ask ourselves, before communicating to the team, why should it matter to them. Why should they embrace the message? It all goes back to purpose. If our people are at the center and heart of our purpose, we have a basis for communicating that message. If our desire is to create a better work environment for our people where they are valued and given a chance to contribute at a high level, then tell them. If our desire is to create a place that people want to be part of the team, then tell them.

2. Set clear expectations that we don't compromise. Consistency and clarity is essential when establishing a culture. Be very clear on how things are ultimately going to work in the process even if there are steps to getting to the final phase of the transformation. You may need to make adjustments along the way, but don't compromise the underlying principles that you conveyed to your team. You can tell that we are using the concept of consistency several times in different applications. That word (*consistency*) must be really important in effectively changing a culture.

3. Narrow the focus. Simplify everything you can down to the basics. The more you can simplify and allow everyone

to understand what's important and how they play a role in the success, the easier it will be to create the culture you want. Eliminate complexity every chance you get. Narrow the overall focus down to the essential elements that you team needs to execute to ensure success. Allow them to focus and own a few things. They need to be able to do these few things very well on a consistent basis. Remove obstacles for them and set them up for success.

4. Emphasize what matters. What the leader talk about the most gets the most attention. Highlight those few things that matter and that the team needs to focus on. Talk about them, provide visual communication of the progress on these items, and ensure that those items are reviewed regularly with team members. Keep the list to no more than three to five items, but make them predominant in the workplace. The focus will ultimately become the norm, and the culture will embrace it. Tell the owners what matters and help them succeed.

5. Practice consistent accountability. Similar to building one's credibility, accountability plays a role in this step too. If we are going to be successful in creating a culture of ownership in the facility, every team player has to do their part. I often use the term *mutual accountability* because there is both responsibility/accountability from leader to follower and follower to leader. This culture is not a soft, passive environment at all, but rather a robust environment that engages everyone at a high level and requires everyone on the team to respond to that challenge.

Those five steps are essentially the action steps for rolling out any form of culture change or process change in a facility or an organization of any type. Once we have built a foundation of credibility with the team, we can successfully share that vision, communicate the why to our team, and start the process of enacting the change in the work environment. It does take time, and the length of time depends on where you are starting from and how complex the change will be to your work environment. Follow the process, and don't skip steps. Trust the process to lead you to success in building a culture of ownership in your organization.

Communicate effectively

If you are going to lead others, you have to be able to communicate. The ability to effectively communicate is the ceiling to your success as a leader. I have previously mentioned that credibility is the foundation to everyone's effectiveness as a leader. That credibility is not always visible, but it must be there for someone to follow you. Conversely, the ability to effectively communicate is very visible and will be a key attribute to your leadership's effectiveness. Whether you view yourself as a public speaker or not is irrelevant, but you have to be able to communicate effectively with the people you lead. If you are going to effectively clarify a vision (see above), you must be able to communicate effectively. Here are a few thoughts on communication for you to consider as you seek to drive culture change in your organization:

1. Communication is more than informing. We too often think of communication as just informing others of information. I want to change that thought process. Effective communication is the transfer of knowledge to another person(s). You can make a verbal announcement or send an email, but you may not have communicated effectively. Whether you are communicating verbally, in writing, or visually, remember, your objective is to transfer knowledge to the target audience.

2. Provide concise and clear messaging. Be sure you know what you are wanting your listener to leave with after you have communicated. Focus your message, limit what you share, and keep the listener in mind. It is better for the listener/follower to leave with one key message than get confused over a lengthy message and leave with nothing. Whether you are speaking or writing, have a clear message

with no more than three key focus items. The objective is to transfer knowledge, not cover information. You aren't checking a box to fulfill some obligation, but rather you are leading your people and need to be effective in communicating to them. You need these people to take action and to know what action is to be taken.

3. Utilize different forms to complement the message. Consistency is not just in the messaging, but in using different forms of communication to both reach different types of learners, as well as to compliment the respective messaging techniques. Provide visual examples of what you talk about and write about. While the message is clear and concise, it can be presented in various forms to emphasize the key concepts. Regardless of the communication type, always seek to clarify and validate understanding. Remember, we are not informing. We are transferring information to another person(s) for use.

4. Narrow the focus and stay centered on the basics. One of the key objectives of any leader, but particularly one interested in building a culture of ownership, is to eliminate complexity and simplify everything possible. That concept is true in communication as well. Narrow your focus to those three things (maybe three to five in some cases) and really focus on those items. The more you talk about a particular item, people will begin to see the importance of that item. The more you write about an item or provide visual communication to that item, people will begin to clearly see what really matters and become more likely to embrace the messaging. Too many key things to focus on just dilutes the information, and no one knows the key information or what really matters. If everything is a priority, there are no priorities.

5. Stay consistent with the message but adapt as needs change. When we constantly change the messaging on a group, we confuse people, complicate the message, and ultimately leave everyone unsure about the direction and

focus of the organization. Consistency is thus very key to effectively communicating with a group over time. With that in mind, there will be times when a leader senses the need to pivot and adapt to a changing environment. When environments change, leaders stay consistent with purpose and conviction but may have to adapt to a new technique or method to continue to be effective in communicating and leading people.

SUMMARY

If you are going to change a culture, you must be a credible leader, provide a clear visions, and you will have to communicate clearly throughout the process of both providing the vision and rolling out your plan for the transformation. Before speaking to a group, writing a message, or posting a chart, always keep the recipient in mind. Just stay focused on the key message or messages that you are seeking to communicate. Narrow the focus, simplify the message, and stay consistent with the focus to ensure your followers are effectively receiving and understanding your key focus areas. Communication is more than just talking. It is planning the message, simplifying the content, utilizing various methods, and validating listener understanding. All of this message has to come from a credible leader though!

THE REST OF THE STORY

Over the years, job assignments would change, but my focus of creating a better workplace for the people remained the same. Culture change was different at every stop along the way due to the inherent environment and current management team's leadership skillset. One thing I can look back on though and be sure of, we always made progress at every stop. Putting forth this effort of culture change to one of ownership was never a waste of time and never one that didn't yield some benefit regardless of the depth that we would reach. I saw examples over the years where the concept was fully embraced and examples where progress was a bit slower but still noticeable in key areas of a facility. Regardless, investing in people and creating a better work environment is always a good thing to work on and one that never stops.

Key learnings:

1. Managers and supervisors stepping up to lead is vital to creating a culture change in any organization.
2. Credibility is the foundation for anyone desiring to lead others.
3. Clarifying a vision of a better place that resonates with the team is key to starting change.
4. Communication ability is the ceiling to any leader's effectiveness.

CHAPTER 4

OWNERS HAVE A NEW IDENTITY

My story

My first day at the national CPA firm was July 5, 1987. I remember that day very distinctly. I had previously interviewed with several of the big eight accounting firms, accepted a job, graduated from college with a degree in accounting, married a young lady I met in school, and moved to South Louisiana in about a six-month time span. I made some huge decisions in a pretty quick time span that would no doubt shape the direction for the rest of my life.

I didn't go to college planning on majoring in accounting, but rather wanted to be a coach. I was drawn to sports my entire life growing up, and I never had really considered doing anything else but coaching. For me, coaching was not just about staying around sports that I loved so much, but rather I always thought it was a great avenue to impact young people. I had witnessed the impact of some very successful coaches back in those days, and I wanted to have that same impact. One coach in particular that really impacted my desire to both coach and invest in others was Grant Teaff. Coach Teaff was the head football coach at Baylor University back in the 1970s and 1980s. He presented at various coach's meetings across the country, spoke at Fellowship of Christian Athlete's events, and wrote several books. I listened to coach Teaff as often as possible and was able to meet him in person when he spoke at my high school football team's awards banquet. I had a clear vision of the path that I wanted to take to impact others.

That plan changed the summer before my freshman year in college. I worked as a teller in a local bank and coached little league baseball at night. Several of the bank executives had boys on the team that I coached, and these men really spent time with me that summer. They took a real interest in me and convinced me that accounting would be a good major for me. They told me that accounting would open up a world of opportunities for me beyond what I could do in coaching. I am not sure how accurate the advice was, but I know they meant well. I grew up in a single-parent home, and we were poor to be honest. My mom worked hard six days a week, and I worked summer jobs since I was twelve years old to help reduce the strain on her. The mentors at the bank convinced me that accounting was my ticket to getting out of poverty and that coaching was not my best route. So I took their advice, went to school, did well in accounting, and landed that job with one of the big eight firms.

Back in those days, those firms were the most prestigious job opportunities for young people graduating in accounting and aspiring to be a certified public accountant. The professors really encouraged students to pursue these opportunities, even if just for a few years of quality work experience. Today, those firms have gone through various mergers and acquisitions, but they still remain highly respected in the field of public accounting and highly thought of on university campuses across the country.

That first day at the CPA firm was thus the culmination of a process that I never anticipated being involved in growing up, but it presented opportunities that I would have never imagined as well. I left early that first morning dressed in one of my three suits that I recently purchased for work. I drove to work in my Chevy Chevette with no air conditioning. In those days, suit and tie at work were the norm regardless of how hot and humid it was in South Louisiana. I was the first one to the office that morning and had to wait outside as I did not have a key to the door yet. My assignments that day and those for the first few weeks were not what I expected. I put money in parking meters for midlevel managers. I hauled equipment and trunks of work papers from vehicles for several managers in the office. I sat in a cubicle for hours reading training materials and getting familiar with software on computers. Portable computers were fairly new to the workplace, and we were all learning how to both use them operationally and effectively as accountants. I would eventually get the opportunity to take several client physical inventories before dawn on most occasions and to start assisting on various client engagements, but my visibility to the firm was very limited. My role was very confined, and I very much looked forward to weekends! As weeks progressed, I was also given the important assignment of being responsible for bringing the keg to Friday after-hour company social events. Being one of the few nondrinkers in the office made me a prime candidate for this assignment. The challenge of being responsible for the keg also meant that I had to stay until everyone was finished in order to return the keg. Those type events really summed up my first year. I was just showing up, doing what I was told, and learning all I could.

I really felt like an outsider most of the time. I wasn't sure if I fit in and if I had made one huge mistake taking a job there. I did pass the CPA exam on my first attempt, and that gave me some job security with the firm and a little more money. Now don't get me wrong, I am no Rhodes Scholar; but I studied hard, got the benefit of the curve on all four parts of that exam, and just barely passed all four parts. I definitely did not overstudy. My certificate looked just like all the other ones though. It still read CPA!

The second year was a little better for me as the assignments increased in responsibility, and the "hazing" type stuff had stopped. There was a new group of accountants that the supervisors and managers were now focused on "developing," and I was a little more involved in generating revenue for the firm. I was still a little uncomfortable with things in the office and still did not have a good grasp of everything that was going on around me.

The big change for me though came in year three. I was promoted to supervisor and actually given responsibility for others. I was invited to attend meetings that before I had only heard about. I was given access to administrative information that allowed me to both know more about our business, our revenue focus, and our overall performance results. For the first time, I now felt like I was an integral part of the firm and was also now communicating with partners of the firm on a regular basis. Just spending time with these individuals provided me the opportunity to both learn at a faster pace but also to take more ownership in what we were doing. That promotion was not just an increase in pay for me. It also changed my entire view of work, my focus at work, and most importantly, my identity at work.

HOW TO CREATE THIS NEW IDENTITY

We don't have to wait for a promotional opportunity to move people toward an ownership mentality in the workplace. We can move them toward that direction by helping create a new identity for them in the work environment within their current role. For those people in supervisory and managerial roles seeking to help others in their new identity, it just requires stepping out of those customary supervisory roles and providing basic leadership direction and input to the team members. We can all get caught up in the busyness of the day and just focus on getting work done. That's an important role for supervisors and managers—to get work done through others. However, leaders are always looking to have impact beyond just their supervisory or managerial responsibilities. Leaders are looking to create fellow owners in the organization and move toward culture change in the workplace to not only create a better working environment but also one that operates more efficiently. The dual win here is that we create an attractive place to work eliminating staffing concerns and also generate sustainable results leading to long-term financial success. Not to mention, we create a really good environment for our people as if that's not motivation enough!

The following are a list of practical ways to help your team members gain this new identity and move toward that ownership mentality in the organization:

1. Owners need purpose. People need to have purpose beyond a paycheck if they are going to be owners. Far too many

workers don't see the bigger picture of what their company or organization is designed to achieve. They don't understand or see the contribution beyond just their specific job assignment. This issue is even more important today as a younger generation of people are more in search of purpose and meaning in their work than prior generations. We need to help all of our team members understand our purpose as a business or organization. Why do we exist? Why are we in business? Who are we ultimately serving? Those are all questions that we need to be able to answer and convey to everyone that works in our organization. People need to see how their individual role or task contributes to this overriding purpose so they too can embrace their personal purpose at work. Every job has value and is important to the purpose of the organization. We just need to communicate more effectively and help others understand their purpose!

2. Owners join the team. They are not hired to do a job. From day one, we need to set the tone for ownership. Not only do we need to convey purpose to them early on, but we need to make a point to bring them in to our organization as team members and not just new hires. We don't need people thinking they were hired but rather given an opportunity to join. That comment may seem like a simple play on words, but it sets the tone for moving one to an ownership mentality early on. The quicker people assimilate with the existing team, gain acceptance, understand purpose, and feel like team members, the faster they take on an ownership mentality. Take a look at your hiring process and see how you can restructure that process to be more ownership focused.

3. Owners need responsibility. If we are going to create owners by giving them a new identity, we have to ensure they both have access to and understand personal responsibility. When people see their role as a responsibility and not just an assigned task, the focus and work take on a whole different meaning. Responsibility leads to accountability and

eventually to that owner mentality that we are seeking to have our people embrace. The key here is to train our people not only on how to perform the job task but also on what they are responsible for regarding the outcome. That approach is a different mindset, but it leads to a different manner in which our people view work and their respective roles at work. By providing opportunities for our people to take on responsibility, we engage them at a higher level, shape that new identity, and move them toward ownership. We need to think beyond the task and convey overall outcome focus to new team members.

4. Owners have an investment. This one may sound a little confusing regarding the workplace. Sure, we all understand the investment when we move toward ownership of a home, a vehicle, or some other tangible possession; but what does ownership in the workplace mean? For our long-standing, tenured employees, they can point toward many years of service as an investment. They are likely very engaged, very committed, and oftentimes available for challenges well beyond the normal job descriptions. In many cases, they do function as owners to the organization. But what about the less senior folks or even the new people that have just joined the team? How can we move them toward that ownership mentality through this concept of needing to invest to own?

First of all, consider building on the responsibility concept shared previously. Take that concept a step further and assign a team member responsibility for an area of the facility. It doesn't matter how large or significant, just ensure they have an area to invest in that everyone knows is their area to maintain. If the organization does not have that physical opportunity, consider assigning a customer or client contact to check in with weekly just to ensure things are going well. It matters less what the customer thinks about the added attention as it does about creating ownership with a new team member.

Anything you can do to create an opportunity to invest in something related to the organization will help.

A second idea is to consider sweat equity investment. Team members that are engaged in a project in the organization from planning to execution and ultimately completion have sweat equity into the project and ultimately the organization. Here, the key is to engage the team members in the entire process and not just use them for labor-focused tasks. The people have to be able to connect the planning and ideation stage with their labor to truly experience the sweat equity approach to investing. Even a seemingly minor project can have big impacts on building a new identity for our people and ultimately leading them toward the ownership mentality. I'll share more on investing later, but just know that investing is a key aspect of developing a new identity at work.

SUMMARY

All of these four concepts or ideas take time and require the leader to invest in people through the end of the transformation process. It is intentional leadership with a purpose in every step along the way. It is not always about being the most efficient or cost effective in the short run, but rather investing in our people to create owners by giving them a new identity. This new identity and subsequent ownership focus will yield sustained results that will far surpass the time and cost invested on the front end. This investment will take time and intentional planning for the leader, but the results will be worth it.

THE REST OF THE STORY

In my fourth year of the firm, all of the midlevel managers in the office resigned within a very short time period. I was able to take on additional responsibility, have expanded influence in the office with junior employees, and actually interact with the managing partner on a regular basis. I will say that year was one of the toughest but most fulfilling years at the firm. I had definitely taken on a new identity and was fully representing the firm and not just doing a job each day. I can now look back and see the impact that I had with other people. I definitely had an unhealthy renter mentality at that firm the first two years; but it came full circle to one of owner mentality when I was given more responsibility, provided access to information, presented with a clearer picture of the purpose, and helped to see my role as something other than just to get work done for someone else. While the promotion and additional responsibilities moved me along in this endeavor, that potential was there in the first two years as well. Neither the structure of the organization nor my response to that structure really provided the opportunity for me to gain this mindset earlier in my time there. The failure to achieve this mindset earlier cost me and the firm some valuable time that could have been mutually beneficial if the ownership concept had been approached early on in my time with the firm. We can move team members toward ownership more efficiently with intentional leadership and planning. This concept takes work, but creating that new identity is a good place to start! It is actually an essential place to start.

Key learnings:

1. Creating an owner identity early on is foundational to moving people toward an owner mentality.
2. We need to make sure we communicate purpose so that people can identify with more than a paycheck as their focus (purpose beyond the paycheck).
3. Quit hiring people and start asking people to join your team.
4. Giving others responsibility starts when we help them see their role is outcome-based not just task focused (training focus is more than how to complete a task but also the expectation of outcome).
5. Leaders have to be intentional with time and focus to direct others to have a new identity and move toward ownership (invest now to yield results later).

CHAPTER 5

OWNERS HAVE ACCESS TO INFORMATION

My story

I t was the mid-1990s, and I was settling into the controller role at the paper mill. The management team at the mill was a very close group and worked very well together. The operations were running pretty well. The safety focus was very strong, and the overall employee engagement level was pretty good throughout the facility. The mill manager was a very visible leader in the facility and frequently challenged the management team on focusing on continual improvement and being more consistent in our execution of the key phases of the process. As we discussed an intentional improvement approach to our operation, we quickly agreed that we had to take the engagement level of our workforce to a deeper level. We had a very experienced group of tenured, skilled workers that were very committed to doing their jobs, but we had not really engaged them beyond that level.

The more we discussed the opportunity to improve overall employee engagement, we quickly determined that we really needed to expand our communication effort and increase our focus in this area. Up to that point, communication efforts were primarily relegated to frontline leaders passing on secondhand information to their crews or employees reading a weekly newsletter that our communication leader would circulate. None of those efforts were bad, and they were pretty consistent with what other mills in our company were doing at the time. However, if we were going to make a step change in engagement, we were going to need to be more strategic in the communication area.

The manager shared with me a booklet of key performance measures (KPMs) that one of the other mills in our company was producing each month. This booklet contained about one hundred KPM graphs with short explanations for each item. There were comments provided on each item that discussed the trend and future focus for improvement. I made some inquiries and discovered that the accounting department in that mill spent about two weeks following their month end close process to produce this booklet and that each department manager in the mill was given a copy. I recall agreeing that KPMs were a great way of focusing and highlighting the keys to our business but that we needed timely information, more focused information, and simplified information presented in a manner for every employee to see and understand. A nice book of KPMs was an impressive presentation, but it would not be that helpful if it wasn't timely and presented in a manner to generate operational change.

The leadership team met to discuss this issue and came away with three overriding metrics that drove our business each day. The success of the business was not easy to achieve, but it was really simple to understand. For one, we had a safety focus of no one getting hurt each day. Secondly, we had a target for tons of paper produced each day. Finally, we had a target for the cost per ton of paper produced. In essence, if we did those three things well, we would run a successful business from an operational perspective. Again, these KPMs were challenging to execute, and it was difficult to reach target levels. But they were not overly complex to understand. There were secondary measures that would be supportive to those items, such as machine reliability percentages, paper quality rates, on-time shipment percentages, and a few others that each of the respective departments would narrow their focus on, as well as they developed their departmental key KPMs. The real key here was that we narrowed the focus down to just a few overriding operational measures that drove success and could be measured timely.

Once these measures were identified, we began discussing the communication effort to ensure we both educated our workforce and kept them informed on an ongoing basis regarding these key measures. We agreed that a multifaceted approach would be the most successful tactic and one that would reach a larger percentage of the workforce. We would communicate verbally in mill-wide meetings with managerial level personnel explaining the focus on how each department and employee played a role in the success. These meetings were short but very focused on the narrow topics and ensured we fully explained the "why" behind each of the measures, as well as why each one was so important to the sustainability of our operation.

We installed TV monitors in key locations throughout the facility and equipped them to present this messaging on a daily basis to keep employees informed of our progress and to provide additional information to aid in further education and increased awareness. We also incorporated a section of the newsletter to provide daily updates in written form for those employees that preferred to read the information. We used charts that were standardized and posted in key areas as well. The key to these charts were simplistic presentation and consistency to enable employees to understand the key messages. Everything was based on the narrow focus and simplified messaging.

Our goal was to improve our communication efforts to better inform our workforce as to what was important. Furthermore, once people were better informed, we could more effectively communicate, build engagement, and get input from those closest to the detail work. The aim was to use information sharing to generate a more consistent focus and to drive continual improvement. They keys to our plan were to narrow the focus, simplify the message, and communicate repetitively with the messaging.

EFFECTIVE COMMUNICATION IS THE CEILING TO A LEADER'S EFFECTIVENESS

While credibility is the foundation to a leader's success, communication is the ceiling to a leader's success. Regardless of the scope of leadership, everyone aspiring to lead others must be able to communicate effectively. I am not saying you have to be the most dynamic public speaker around, but you have to be able to effectively communicate with people within your scope of responsibility. If you can't communicate effectively, you can't lead effectively.

So what is communication? Far too often, we think of communication as just informing people or providing information. Effective communication in the workplace is much more than just informing. Informing may not be enough. I have gone through far too many post-incident safety investigations over the years where the safety manager tells me that the information was shared in a video training exercise three years ago, and evidently the individual just didn't listen. So someone is seriously hurt, and we fall back on the fact that we "told them not to" as our basis for not taking responsibility. For some reason, that communication effort was not effective, and that excuse tells us more about the effectiveness of our training and communication plans than we want to admit.

Communication has to be more than just informing. Communication has to be the transfer of knowledge and awareness to another person(s). That definition provides an entirely different view of communication and moves us from just checking the box as a supervisor or manager to the role of a leader aspiring to have influence with a team. That role of leader having influence and taking responsibility for the message gives communication a very different meaning.

As we seek to move our team members to an ownership mentality and change the culture of the workplace, we have to realize that owners have access to information. It is thus essential that leaders be equipped to effectively communicate at all levels and through various mediums to ensure our prospective "owners" have this access to information that they both understand and find relevant. The following concepts will provide you with some key insights on how to effectively communicate with your team and provide them with access to key information.

1. Communication needs to be clear, concise, and timely. Now that we have clarified that communication is more than just informing but rather the transfer of information to another person(s), let's focus on how to be effective in this key area. To ensure we are clear and concise, we always need to ensure we have narrowed the focus to begin any discussion. Narrowing the focus is reducing our message down to no more than three key messages in any communication effort. The listener is often overwhelmed with too much content and is not likely to take action if the message isn't understood and retained. By narrowing the focus and clarifying our message, we are much more likely to actually transfer that knowledge to the listener. A clear, concise message with the appropriate level of repetition of the key message in the delivery will go a long way to effectively transferring this information to the listener.

   Couple that approach with a timely delivery of the content, and we will be much more successful in providing our workforce with information to aid in culture change and overall awareness of important focus areas. Timely messaging is often an overlooked attribute of effective communication, timely addresses when the recipient is in a high state of acceptance or readiness to hear the message. The focus of any message being communicated has to be the hearer or recipient. The message has to be clear, concise, and delivered in a timely manner to be effective. We achieve these factors by narrowing the focus, being repetitive in the messaging, and being timely with our listener's needs in mind. Always go into any communication effort with a clear picture of what you want the audience to learn from the discussion.

2. Communication is also active listening. Far too often, we think our role as managers and supervisors is to do all the talking as we provide direction to others. There is some truth in that assumption, but when we step out of those basic supervisory roles and begin to actually lead others, we will also need to effectively listen to those people that we are leading. Listening to others provides benefit to leaders in multiple ways. When we listen to others, we can validate that our message was understood by asking listeners to clarify what they have heard and to repeat what they need to do differently. By listening to others, we can also gain perspective of what's going on within the workforce and our team members. The old concept of managing by walking around and investing time with people is a great way to be present and listen to our people. A leader taking time to listen to people in their respective work areas is a priceless investment for any leader. The information obtained and understanding achieved is so valuable for the leader both short term and long term. We may learn by listening to our team that we need to make adjustments in our communication approach to be more effective. Remember, we aren't just informing, but rather we are transferring information to the listener with the intent to equip them to be more successful and ultimately be an "owner" in the business. Owners have access to information, and we have to listen to ensure we are providing access to that information effectively.

3. Communication is both verbal and visual. Effective verbal communication transfers knowledge when people hear and understand what we are saying. Effective visual communication transfers knowledge when people see and understand what we present. These visuals presentations can be charts, graphs, notes, memos, etc. The most effective approach is to have these various modes of communication complement one another. Narrowing our focus to a few key messages and presenting those messages in differ-

ent forms will provide us the most effective opportunity to achieve our goal of effectively transferring knowledge to our team and to provide the desired access to information that an ownership mentality would contain.

4. Questions are a great way to communicate. Most leaders don't fully utilize the power of asking good open-ended questions. We often think of asking questions to just gain information or obtain clarification from someone. Questions can also be used by a leader to have influence. Leaders influence others through the use of open-ended questions by getting the listener to actively think, to thoughtfully process through a response, and then to clearly articulate a response. That three-step process will strengthen one's ability to retain information that we are providing them. That process will also strengthen the engagement level in the conversation and enhance the quality of the two-way dialogue, leaving the listener with a much-improved retention rate of the subject matter.

SUMMARY

Regardless of the leadership topic being discussed, communication is an essential element. A leader must be able to effectively communicate a vision to be achieved, the process to be followed, a change to be implemented, or any number of key things to be accomplished at different times. The keys are always to narrow the focus to aid in retention, create an environment conducive for the listener to understand, be concise to maintain attention, and be repetitive to drive home the key messages. If we are going to move people from a renter mentality to an owner mentality, we must make information available to our people. We have to be more open with information but also very strategic in how we package and present the information to our people. Remember, we are not just dumping information on them but rather looking for approaches to effectively transfer knowledge to them. This information is to not only direct how work is done but also to help move people to an owner mentality with the increased access to that information.

THE REST OF THE STORY

We had significant success in simplifying our business communication and sharing it more broadly and more timely. Some of the keys to this success were us narrowing the focus to just a few KPMs and targeting our communication strategy to use a variety of methods to complement one another all aimed at a consistent message to the workforce. We were also able to achieve this focus effort with timely delivery of the information. The resulting benefits were multilayered. We saw a significant increase in improvement ideas generated from those performing the detail work. We also saw increased engagement levels, increased communications between supervisors and workers, and an improvement in the overall results that we were focused on.

One thing that really stood out was the benefit we saw when we told people what was important, how we were doing, and how they could help made a big impact. I was surprised at the response from some long-standing employees that had so much to share. I had conversations that would have never taken place had we not engaged in this intentional communication effort. While some of these conversations with employees were often just focused on clarifying why we were doing certain things, there were other conversations that really led to some great cost-reduction ideas and process-improvement suggestions. In addition, the value of the increased engagement likely went far beyond what we could clarify in a standard process-improvement report.

Now we didn't have the concept of ownership at that time, but we simply focused on driving engagement through improved communication. The success of this effort really provided the background for ensuring that we included this access to information as part of our process in moving a team toward improved engagement in the workplace. Owners have access to information, and if we are going to move team members toward ownership, leaders must communicate effectively to ensure we provide that accesses to the information.

Key learnings:

1. Communication is the ceiling to the success level for any leader.
2. Communication is more than just informing. It is the successful transferring of information to another person(s).
3. Narrowing the focus to no more than three key messages helps us be clear and concise in our communication.
4. Timely communication focuses on the listener to ensure we achieve relevance and attention of the recipient.
5. The effective use of open-ended questions and active listening can be key tools for enhancing communication efforts with your team.

CHAPTER 6

OWNERS TAKE INITIATIVE

My story

Looking back at my first general manager role in the 1990s and the transformation effort that I have previously discussed, I distinctly recall one of the key initiatives that we undertook to improve our operation. Our goal was to engage our team members to take more initiative in all aspects of the business to both drive improvements and to change the culture in our facility. During those first few months, I had spent long hours developing and implementing systems, getting the right leadership team in place, and repairing relationships with customers (remember the Apology and Recommitment Tour from chapter 1). Once we had those foundational elements established, we began the process of transforming the culture in the facility.

One of the key transformational areas we had to address was that of initiative. I found myself carrying way too much of the load in making decisions, resolving problems, eliminating obstacles, and changing the culture. My initial efforts to engage key leaders in the plant to assist me in this effort was still not enough. We would not make the progress that was needed nor reach the performance levels that were possible unless we got others involved in a broader and more focused manner. Now that would be a challenge with a workforce that was previously largely disengaged and had little to no experience doing anything more than just what they were told to do by their supervisor.

I needed to communicate very clearly and convey the benefits to everyone of this desire to get everyone more involved in taking initiative and not to rely on me to be the key to our success. An over-reliance on one leader is a dangerous and limiting factor for any organization. That type of reliance not only puts a great deal of pressure on that leader. It also limits the organization's potential for success based on the ability level of that one leader. For an organization to reach its potential, it needs everyone contributing at a high level with ideas, solving problems, and expanding their respective roles in the mission.

Beyond just establishing this need, I also needed this communication effort to be impactful and for us to follow up with specific actionable items to drive this plan forward to ensure it was successfully implemented. Other managers and frontline leaders would need to fully grasp the concept if we were going to have success, and they too would have to increase their level of involvement and initiative as well. The first step in the process was a short plant-wide meeting with each of the three shifts. I spent about fifteen to twenty minutes with each of the shifts in our training room with just a single key message—the need for everyone to take initiative and start approaching their jobs as if they were the owners. That concept was something very new for the majority of the workforce and not something common in an operation of our size or our industry.

I brought a football with me for a visual aid in this discussion. I recall telling the team members that I was carrying the ball far too much. If I continued to carry the ball all the time, we would never be any better than where my talents and abilities would take us. If on the other hand, everyone took that ball on occasion, our ceiling to success would be raised, and we could develop a workplace that they had never seen before. It may sound silly, but I let them pass that ball around the room with each one getting a chance to hold it for just a second or two. As symbolic as that might have been, it was a visual picture of what we needed to achieve. It was a symbol that we all had something to contribute and that we would be better with everyone engaged at a higher level. That transition though would take acceptance and a willingness to step out of long-standing views of work for the majority of our workforce. While the opportunities sounded appealing, change was never easy. It is one thing to help a group take on a new identity and to provide more access to information, but getting them to take more initiative is the first real step for the team members to actually do something different. You need to lay the foundation, but there does come a time for people to actually do things differently.

Those three meetings went well, and we quickly moved to phase two of the initiative. This phase was focused on taking this message and putting it into action. It is also one thing to share a visionary message in a meeting with a visual aid but quite another to go and start taking action on that vision. We started by increasing the role of our supervisory personnel who served as frontline leaders for our workforce. We clearly outlined their roles and enhanced their decision-making authority and provided them some hands-on training and development opportunities to assist them with this expanded influence and role in the facility. Some of the key areas we focused on were giving them some input on order scheduling, preventative maintenance scheduling, vacation management for their shift, and various process-improvement-focus areas. Each supervisor was also given a special focus area of the plant or unique process within the plant to assume responsibility and accountability. By enhancing the focus, we would both raise the inherent value of the leader and create an atmosphere for more personal initiative to take place. They quickly embraced the expanded role concept, took the initiative that was afforded to them, and started making an impact on each of the three shifts.

Once we were comfortable with that group taking on a larger role and ensured that it was visible in the facility (everyone needed to see that we were actually taking action from those plant-wide meetings), we then moved our focus to the senior operators in the facility. I really liked this group and was confident that we could be successful elevating their roles. This group had stuck it out during some tough times with prior management teams and were a pretty seasoned group of skilled operators. They were influential with other team members in the facility, and getting them on board would be a key move in getting others to take initiative.

We talked about some ideas on how to expand their role, their influence, and ultimately received some great ideas from them as they shared some thoughts on how they could contribute further. Some of the key areas we focused on with them were allowing them to help determine machine performance goals for the respective machines within a department, to enter and prioritize maintenance needs for their machine, to be involved with new hire orientation, training, and evaluation, and to develop their own organization approach for supplies and materials in their respective machine areas. We also wanted this group to be much more engaged with corporate visits, customer visits, and our overall visibility in the community. I will say that this group embraced those items much quicker and much better than I had expected. This group was largely first shift operators as a result of most of the senior personnel wanting to be on day shift. I had a chance to watch them in action and see the impact that they were having not only within their crews but also with the other shifts. They quickly accepted the expanded roles and achieved more than I could have ever expected in such a short time period.

The final phase was to take this concept to the rest of the work-force across the facility. By this time, the concept was fully engrained and largely accepted. We were already seeing elements of employee initiative taking place in various parts of the facility. We merely needed to help promote the concept and find ways to help people see where they could take initiative in their respective work areas to make an impact. To aid in this awareness and to generate some additional focus around this concept, we developed some "make a difference" (MAD) posters and placed them at strategic areas throughout the facility. The idea was to further draw attention to process opportunities to make a difference for one's coworker, our customers, or our facility in general. We strategically posted these MAD ideas close to key quality points in our process and key safety focus areas. By getting more people focused on taking care of customers and taking care of each other, we would be driving engagement in two key primary focus areas for our operation. I was surprised at just how many people got on board and took the initiative as a result of our just making them aware of the importance of everyone taking such initiative and helping them see where they could make an impact.

RESPONSIBILITY IS MORE THAN A JOB ASSIGNMENT

Most people would associate the concept of taking responsibility at work with fulfilling the obligations of one's job assignment. Likewise, when we prepare a listing of job duties, annual objectives, or position descriptions on the organizational chart, we do so to provide a general framework for the job and the associated expectations within those job assignments. There is no doubt that this type of framework is helpful in the hiring, training, and performance review processes for many companies. The problem with an overreliance on these approaches is that while they define things clearly, they can also limit the impact of an individual and can do more harm than good to an organization. Have you ever heard the term "that's not my job?" Wonder where that phrase came from? I bet a clearly presented and narrowly defined job description being followed to the letter of the law was the source of that comment. That focus is in direct contrast to a culture of ownership where team members take initiative well beyond a specific job task.

When moving team members to an ownership mentality in the workplace, we need to expand that understanding of responsibility beyond just a narrowly focused job description. Owners are not limited to a finite-focused list of assignments. Owners have a broader view of their role and the scope of their overall level of responsibility. Sure, team members have specific duties that have to be accomplished, but they take initiative well beyond those defined duties. We have to move beyond the typical organizational charts and job descriptions to move our people to an ownership mentality in our organization. We have to remove the standard limitations and unleash our people to contribute beyond those limitations, and when we do, we can then expect more from everyone in the process.

Far too often, we lean too much on that structural approach and need to learn to lead beyond the organizational chart. Whether we are talking about the roles of supervisors, managers, or frontline workers, we need to realize these individuals have unique skillsets, experiences, and passions that can help our organization in any number of ways. While we need to effectively define and execute our process, we also need to provide our people the freedom to do what they do best within the framework of the process and not limit initiative taking within our team. The key is finding that balance between the execution of a well-structured process and the flexibility within that structure to allow our team members to flourish and contribute in their unique ways. The following are some practical approaches to consider when making this transformation.

1. Clearly define the job assignment but broaden the responsibility. We do need to clearly define and explain what we need each person to focus on in any organization. We will never get away from clearly defining the keys to each task and what must be accomplished to be successful in any role within our organization. However, let's don't stop with that initial job-specific training. We need to also expand the overall responsibility beyond specific job assignment to the overall needs of the organization. There is no limit to responsibility as we all need to view our role as joint owners. Owners are not limited in the level of responsibility and take initiative wherever the need arises.

2. Accountability is responsibility's close friend. Accountability is defined as the acceptance of responsibility. If we want to instill responsibility and initiative in our team, we have to couple that with accountability. We have to set expectations to that level and not just hope it will take hold. Accountability provides the substance to responsibility and ultimately the expectation for taking initiative. Without implied and clarified accountability associated with increased responsibility, we will oftentimes fall short in execution. Accountability can take on many different forms

and does not have to violate basic human resource policies if these areas of responsibility fall outside the normal scope of work but can be one of both leader and peer expectations for the team. Most people don't want to let their coworkers down or disappoint those they work with on a daily basis. If we can be timely and consistent in holding one another accountable for taking responsibility, we can be effective in driving culture change in the organization.

3. Start small, but start early. It's key to encourage our people to take full responsibility for the operation from day one. Beginning with this key principle as a foundational aspect of our culture will enable us approach this item on several fronts. While we would focus cultural change with senior members initially, we could also include this approach in our onboarding process with new hires as well. We would obviously start with small, targeted areas of responsibility and expand as the individual gains understanding of the business and overall goals of the operation. By instilling a mindset of responsibility for the organization as a whole at the start, conveying an understanding of accountability for everything that happens, and providing an overall mindset of taking initiative in the workplace, we can effectively move our team toward an ownership mentality.

4. Engage and include your team. Far too often, we miss opportunities to include our team members in key activities such as participating in corporate personnel visits, leading facility tours, meeting with customers either in our facility or at customer locations, and other events often reserved for key managerial personnel. With a little preparation, many of our team members can effectively function and take responsibility for various aspects of these types of events. Not only does this type of inclusion increase ownership focus, but it also presents a very engaged workforce to corporate personnel and customers. Trust me, customers love to hear directly from those responsible for making their products. I have heard several customers comment to

me that they really appreciate hearing from the production employees as to their commitment level. These interactions not only strengthen our message and provide credibility to the organization. They also instill the key message to our team member involved. Allowing our team members to interact directly with those outside our organization goes a long way to increasing our people's view of responsibility and ultimately taking initiative and ownership in the workplace.

SUMMARY

As we think about encouraging our team members to take more initiative, we need to consider creating an atmosphere that drives people to be more responsible and to take personal accountability beyond just their normal work tasks. We need to promote broader-based thinking of accomplishment of a complete process rather than just individually task focused. Sure, we execute at the task level, but we promote responsibility and accountability at a broader level of thinking. When we get to this type of cultural focus, we are well on our way to having our team members take initiative and become owners in our organization. That's a pathway to sustained culture change.

THE REST OF THE STORY

Looking back at that initial effort to lead others to seek responsibility, accept accountability, and ultimately pursue initiative outside of their specific job tasks, I consider that focused effort to have been one of the more impactful cultural change events that we accomplished. Providing the opportunity for team members to be involved in the business beyond their historically limiting job task assignment really opened up the workforce's contribution level beyond what we had ever seen in the past. We saw engagement go to a new level. We saw discretionary effort increase and process improvement not just increase but also those initiatives be sustained in subsequent periods.

Outside visitor and customers were able to engage our employees at various levels of the operation and interact directly with them on many occasions. Allowing our employees to better understand our customer's operations had a meaningful impact on our service, quality, and overall team member initiative related to supporting those customer needs.

One may ask if there were any setback or problems in this approach. Yes, there were occasional issues where poor decisions were made, performance was lacking, or comments in the wrong environment were made. However, there was nothing that we could not correct, overcome, or address effectively. The issues were expected and understandable given the changes we were implementing. The short and long-term benefits far exceeded these isolated negative encounters though.

In addition, some may ask how this approach would work in a union environment. Keep in mind, we aren't requiring or mandating anything but rather creating an environment that expands team member's opportunities to have input and "ownership." Implementing such a strategy does not change the manner in which people are paid or represented in the workplace, but rather just elevates the value of each team member and elevates the ceiling on what can be achieved. Leaders can implement this approach in any type of environment. Culture change is about people and not about representation methods.

As I look back on our move toward an ownership mentality in the work environment, I can now see more clearly how that progression from responsibility to accountability and ultimately to an increase in personal initiative was an essential element in our pursuit of employee ownership. Owners are not limited in scope, but rather take initiative and seek a more holistic view of the process. While team members may question more things, these questions can generate improvement and result in some great conversations among fellow "owners." Sure, it takes more time on the part of the leader to push responsibility to others to ultimately drive initiative taking in the organization, but the future benefits far exceed the upfront costs of time. It also requires trust on the part of the leader, but here again, you would be surprised at what our people can do with the proper leadership and guidance. If we want to create a culture of ownership, we have to lead well and provide an environment for others to take initiative and assume responsibility.

Key learnings:

1. Responsibility is more than a job description.
2. Balance a structured process with flexibility within the process to allow people to flourish.
3. Define the roles clearly, but broaden the responsibility to encourage initiative.
4. Accountability is the substance that makes responsibility meaningful.
5. Start early, engage broadly, and expand roles as people grow.

CHAPTER 7

OWNERS HAVE INPUT

My story

During my first general manger assignment back in the 1990s, we were making progress, instilling a sense of initiative with our team members, and they were taking more personal and team responsibility in the facility. As the leadership team discussed the next step to take in our move toward a workplace culture of ownership, it was apparent that we had to get more input for some of the decision-making and enable our people to have more involvement on key decisions. Owners obviously have input, and we needed to identify an approach that would allow our people to have input, but to do so in a manner that was efficient and effective. The benefits were twofold. We would engage our people to move toward a culture change of ownership and gather good input to make better decisions for our business.

The challenge with getting more input for the decision-making is that just getting popular opinion on key business decisions is not the most effective way to run a business, nor is it practical. We can't put every key decision out for vote, nor do we have the time to approach decision-making in that manner. There are far too many decisions to be made each day on customer needs, spending issues, personal matters, or any other number of items that come up every day in a business. It is just not practical to take the time to fully explain all angles to a group on every issue that comes up in the course of the day. Every business has to be organized in a manner to make solid decisions in a timely manner while looking out for the best interests of their business and their team members.

With that in mind though, we had to find an approach to allow our team members to have more input. As we discussed this matter, it became apparent that while we couldn't decentralize everything in the facility regarding decision-making, we could carve out small but meaningful items and allow our team members to be involved to a degree. One of the initial steps we took was to designate approximately 5 percent of our facility spending budget each month and allow our first shift operators, along with a senior member of our maintenance department, to decide how this money would be spent each month. These individuals were the most tenured and respected team members in the facility. The money would have to be used to upgrade some aspect of the facility, and the spending had to fully comply with corporate purchasing policy requirements.

Our goal was to have these senior representatives talk to workers in their respective departments and across the different shifts through the month and then get together to decide where they felt the money could be most effectively used in the facility. As long as the suggestion was within policy, we wanted to honor their request and take their input. While it was not a great deal of money, 5 percent of a tight budget was significant enough to make the discussions meaningful and still allow for us to operate effectively while getting our people more involved in having input in the facility.

The second major focus area that we modified to allow our team members to have input on was the prioritization of maintenance work orders on their machines. While the final decision would continue to rest with the maintenance manager and production manager, we definitely wanted and needed operator input in this manner. It was an opportunity for us to provide our operators with the ability to have more input and to gather better information from these operators regarding opportunities to improve our productivity and to reduce our waste.

Here again, we would work through the first shift operators to obtain input from the various operating crews across all three shifts. These operators were briefed periodically regarding open work orders on their respective machines. They were asked to solicit input from other shifts and crew members and come to the maintenance planning meeting (weekly meeting) to provide input as to their preference on priorities. We had a very tight maintenance spending budget and were limited on personnel resources at times as well. It was therefore critical that we prioritized spending and machine downtime carefully to have the most impact as possible with respect to operational improvement. Getting input from operating personnel in an efficient and timely manner would not only help us make better decisions with respect to prioritization, but it would engage the operating personnel and be another step toward moving them to an ownership mentality and changing the culture in our facility.

INPUT BEYOND THE SUGGESTION BOX

Several years ago, our company went through a very extensive employee engagement effort across the entire workforce. The initial phase of this effort was a survey questionnaire given to each employee with just some basic engagement questions. When the survey came back, we were instructed to meet with individual work teams, review the results, and develop an action plan to build on the strengths and address the biggest weaknesses that were noted from the survey results. It was pretty standard approach, and I was very glad to see our company investing so much in building engagement and focusing on our people across the company. The power of an engaged workforce is something often underestimated, and the benefits of such are both business oriented, as well as people-based.

I was not surprised that the results of the survey were very similar company wide as they were for our facility. Our biggest opportunity dealt with employee's opinions mattering to the management team. For far too long, the workforce was just asked to come do their job and let others make all the decisions for the facility. It was not surprising at all that a large percentage of employees felt as if their opinion didn't matter to management. People have ideas, concerns, and generally want to be able to express themselves in a manner that makes a difference. We now had survey results that validated that assumption, and it was time to take action.

While it was obvious what needed to be addressed, the targeted action to resolve the opportunity was not necessarily that clear. I contacted quite a few other facilities and visited many of these places as well to see how they were addressing the issue. The predominant approach was a suggestion box placed in the plant. This box was geared to be an efficient, anonymous method to allow employees to express concerns and suggestions to management. I witnessed several of these boxes installed in facilities and even noticed that some were padlocked. To be honest, I thought it was a terrible idea. If we were going to make meaningful progress on developing a system to allow employees to have input and for that input to meaningfully change workplace culture, it was going to take more than placing a box in the plant. I am not sure why some added the anonymous approach and placed locks on the boxes. I assume there were managers that were afraid someone was going to steal those suggestions. I also noted that many facilities would go weeks without checking these boxes. I am sure the delays in checking the box created negative views by the workforce. In addition, many of the facilities failed to install a feedback system associated with the suggestion box approach. Thus, employees had no clear path to receive feedback on their suggestion which I am certain had a negative impact and likely validated the view that that their opinions really didn't matter after all. Those suggestion boxes likely did more harm than good in many cases and were a failure.

So let's move beyond the quick fix of the suggestion box and really deal with employee engagement and input. Employee input and opinions are a dynamic part of the business and can't be captured in a box. Real engagement is continuous dialogue within a culture of open discussion, idea sharing, and feedback. We won't see the full benefit of increased interaction with our team members and their sharing input on key issues until it becomes a normal course for our operation. For our people to trust us and see value in providing input, particularly where on open environment of team member input hasn't taken place in the past, it will take some time. The following are some suggestions that you can utilize to build this engagement, obtain this input, and move toward an ownership culture that we all need in today's workplace.

1. Seek input regularly and avoid a gripe session. If you only seek out employee opinions occasionally, you are likely to be met with a lot of complaints and hostility from employees during these discussions. Those feelings of not being listened to get worse over time and will be unleashed when given the opportunity. If you want to avoid that type of feedback, don't have "events" but rather establish a system of regular input and interaction so the discussions are more balanced and inclusive in the normal course of business. Now you will still have complaints being voiced from time to time, but the approach will provide you a much better system of interaction and feedback. To be most effective, we need to think ongoing communication system and not feedback events.

2. Open the doors to relevant discussions. We have all heard the term *open-door policy* and know what that generally means. I have seen people say they have an open-door policy in their facility or place of business only to walk in and see doors closed all the time. I have seen access to certain offices restricted to only certain personnel, but we still claim to operate with an open-door policy. If we really want to engage and provide an opportunity for our team members to have input, include people in meetings where they can add value. Include an hourly production employee in a maintenance planning meeting to help prioritize needs. Include a shipping employee in a customer service meeting to ensure communication is clear on customer priorities. Include a key maintenance person in a capital planning meeting when discussing future projects. You can do any number of these things by letting influential team members

represent their department and have not only a seat at the table but a voice too. You would be surprised at the meaningful input obtained after a few rounds of this approach.

3. Meals are a great time to talk. I have found that weekly lunch or dinner meals with five or six people from the workforce are great opportunities to engage in conversation in a very informal, relaxed environment. There is something natural about just talking and sharing ideas together over a meal. Everyone is going to take time to eat anyway, so why not plan a regular meal with rotating groups of people to talk? The expense of providing a meal for a small group is not that significant and is not an additional commitment on the leader's part either. Everyone is going to take the time to eat, so why not make an investment of that time once a week with your team? You can meet the entire workforce over a short period of time and establish an effective communication approach to gather input from those wanting to share ideas. People are not forced to provide input, but they are sure given the opportunity.

4. Teams are powerful. If you want to take engagement and gathering input to a higher level, get employees involved with improvement teams. The key here is to provide solid leadership to each team until they can be self-sustaining, but give them as much authority with respect to their mission as possible. You may engage in some activities early on that don't yield great results, but that's part of the team-building process. Your people need to see you entrusting them with the mission and purpose of the team. Be clear with the mission, guide in the early stages, and ease out when the team is self-sustaining. There's not a more powerful way to provide team members with the ability to have input than turning opportunities over to them to solve.

5. There are bad ideas. Providing an opportunity for our people to have input and express opinions doesn't mean we have to do everything that is brought up or suggested. I have heard a lot of really bad ideas over the years. I know

some will say in a brainstorming session that there are no bad ideas. Whoever said that has not heard some of the stuff that I have heard over the years. While we want to encourage input and feedback, we also have a responsibility to lead well and make good decisions for our followers. There will be times that we have to go a different direction or redirect the focus. Leaders can redirect without shutting down the conversation or hurting the engagement level.

SUMMARY

As we work through these opportunities to help our team members share their input, it becomes very obvious how much we really value our people. If we truly do value them for not only what they do but also what they think, it makes this process of gaining input much easier. If we value them, we want to hear from them and get their input. It just seems like a natural course of events to want input from those we value. By soliciting their input, we build engagement and move them toward that ownership mentality. Owners have input, and it's our role to develop an approach and an atmosphere to facility that input sharing.

THE REST OF THE STORY

Looking back, we did a variety of things to build engagement and get team members input. All of them were helpful to an extent and added value at the time. We used task teams for process improvement items that were geared to a specific item in a defined period of time. Our people responded very well to these initiatives and offered great input and insight. We had rotating team members participate in various meetings, and that added value beyond what I would have ever expected. We had the "dining with Doug" for a period of time that allowed me to talk over a thirty-minute meal break with a small group of team members. Those were outstanding opportunities for me to get to know people on all shifts. I did have to get comfortable eating at some odd times though with that third shift group. One of the most successful initiatives was holding a one-to-one session with each employee where I spent about twenty minutes just talking with them and getting their ideas and input on anything they wanted to discuss. I left these discussions with plenty of notes and things to follow up on to address their concerns. Those discussion were so valuable, and I strongly suggest investing in those one-to-one sessions to anyone leading people. The sessions do take time, but the benefits are enormous! One mistake I did make is doing one round of those one-to-one sessions in a twenty-four-hour straight period with no sleep. While the commitment level to the employee group was obvious, I am not sure how effective I really was in the later hours of that session. I am not sure how much I got out of that twenty-four-straight employee discussions, but people were talking about it for weeks. If nothing else, they knew their facility leader was committed to the team and could go a day without sleep!

Overall, we really excelled in this area as much as any area we focused on in building engagement and moving our culture to one of team member ownership in the workplace. I'm sure we weren't perfect in execution all the time, but the benefits of getting people involved to provide input far exceeded our expectations. If I had it to do again, I would have gone after this element in the process much sooner as it provided our leadership team with a lot of credibility in our efforts to change culture.

Key learnings:

1. Input is more than a suggestion box and really takes us to the heart of valuing our people.
2. Seek input regularly and avoid creating feedback events that can turn negative.
3. An open-door policy is more than a statement.
4. Have meals with your people to promote interaction and use teams to facilitate problem-solving and engagement.
5. There are bad ideas, so be prepared.

CHAPTER 8

OWNERS ARE INQUISITIVE

My story

As we made progress in moving our facility toward one with an ownership culture, it also became apparent to us that we needed our people to start paying more attention to details and to be more inquisitive of the various processes in our operation. As we made progress addressing the major items, we now could start working on what were originally less significant issues that were now rising higher on our priority list. While we always wanted to stay narrowly focused on a few key variables to drive the operation, we also knew that doing the little things well at the operator level would really pay off. We could only do these seemingly little things well if we encouraged our people to be more inquisitive, to challenge things that didn't look right and ultimately to pay attention to details on key aspects of our operation.

We desperately wanted to take several of our operational systems to higher levels of performance, and improved execution was going to be the key in achieving that goal. Recall that we define *strategy* as asking ourselves if we are doing right things. We define *execution* as asking ourselves if we are doing things right. Those two concepts and definitions have to work together to achieve success. The same words in a different order provide a very different view but complement one another perfectly. We were comfortable with our strategy and operating plan with respect to the key areas of safety, quality, and reliability but still had opportunities to improve our consistency in the execution phase. The key here would be to strengthen that execution through building engagement with our people, finding ways to encourage team members to be more inquisitive, and educating these folks on the value of details. We needed to get everyone realizing that little things done well over time would make a big difference. We believed that the increased focus would be the key to more consistent execution in all three of those key operational areas.

It would be easy just to say we were going to be more direct in our management approach and just hold people more accountable to drive this focus. If that statement means we are going to use discipline to be the enforcer, I would say to get comfortable with that approach if that's what you want to do. While discipline and accountability always have a place in any business operation, if that's the basis for driving execution, then that method will likely always be the approach. I have seldom seen a facility base their plan on discipline exclusively and be able to transition to another approach as a result of the resounding success with the disciplinarian approach. Once discipline is the primary basis for executing well, it will always be required because there is no other motivation involved. It is a very negative avoidance method. We are much more successful when we can engage and motivate our folks to perform for positive reasons rather than just to avoid punishment. Now to clarify, discipline and accountability are always a part of any leadership system, but they are not the primary or sole approach used.

With that positive approach in mind, we did a few things that would seem pretty different for most people running a business of any type but particularly out of the ordinary for those running a manufacturing facility. We transformed my office into an engagement-focused room as opposed to a typical general manager office. We moved the desk and associated furniture out and replaced those items with a midsized conference table with an ample number of chairs around it. We placed a white board and a flip chart in the office to facilitate our plan on getting our people more engaged, more inquisitive, and more aware of paying attention to key details in our processes.

With our focused narrowed to safety, quality, and productivity, we went back to our workforce and had the team members select a representative from each department on each shift to be on the revamped safety committee. While participation would be voluntary on this team, we wanted a cross section of team members representing the entire facility. This team would help us focus on details within our safety system that would often go overlooked until we had an occurrence that required us to investigate and take action. Our thinking was that we could empower this team to have an impact in the facility that would go well beyond what our EHS manager could do on his own. Our EHS manager was an outstanding leader of people and did a terrific job bringing this team together. He related to people so well that we had no problem getting team members to serve on this committee. This team would display their key focus areas on the white board in our new engagement room (where I also worked with my laptop and phone) so that we could both see their initiatives and monitor their progress.

Secondly, we asked the operating crews to also select a representative to take responsibility for getting input from all shifts on the most concerning issues related to their respective machines that were causing quality or productivity issues. They would write these three to five opportunities on the flip chart (page designated for each machine) located in my revamped office area. Our leadership team would meet every morning around the table in this new office/engagement room, and we would discuss how we were going to address those issues noted on the flip charts. The issues would stay on the flip chart page until the representative acknowledged that the issue was resolved and marked it off. The representative could then add another item to the page when appropriate. No one else could take the item off the page because we had to do a better job of communicating when problems were resolved on our machines. While we would place completed work order information on machines, it was not always clear to team members on the machine that the actual problem was resolved. It is one thing to complete a work order (task) and quite another thing to resolve a problem. By empowering our designated team members to be the only ones that could take an item off the list on the flip chart, we ensured that the problem was actually resolved, not just that the work order was completed. Having operators come into my work area throughout the day to update these postings was another excellent opportunity for me to engage them in conversation.

We attacked those three key areas (safety, quality, and productivity) in this manner by getting our people more engaged and more focused on the details. We had to get them to be more inquisitive of problems and challenges rather than just relying on supervision to continually challenge things and resolve problems. The more people that were involved and engaged in problem-solving provided us a better opportunity to achieve the desired results.

Another unexpected occurrence happened during this time frame that we did not expect, and it provided another unplanned opportunity. Our maintenance manager resigned as a result of a family situation. His wife had a terrific job opportunity in another city, and he decided to follow her. With this change coming as a surprise to us and no one clearly identified to take his place, we decided to make a move and break down some departmental walls that we felt were hindering our progress. We took our maintenance department and divided them amongst the operating departments and had these team members report directly to those departmental leaders for a period of time. There was something to be said of everyone having the same goals, working closely together, and getting the same directional message every day even with different skillsets and job focus. That step, while not intending to be long term, did promote dialogue and attention to details within our operating departments. Communication between operating personnel and maintenance personnel increased as they were one team now with just different roles on the team. People began asking more questions and gaining a better understanding of the different roles and needs in the plant. I really enjoyed walking through the facility and seeing team members from different departments and different skill sets working so well together. It was great to see everyone aligned and working in one direction!

YOU GET WHAT YOU EXPECT

If we want our team members to pay more attention to details and to be more inquisitive about issues with the operation, we have to both model and to expect that type of behavior. Paying attention to detail is not the norm in most operations without a focused effort to drive people toward that direction. A positive, engaging focused approach is always more sustainable than just a punitive discipline-based approach when directing this effort. Similar to leading other key initiatives in a facility or organization, we are always more successful on a sustained basis if we can get people believing in what we are doing rather than just avoiding negative consequences. We must take the time to have influence and not just provide direction. Influence is going beyond telling others what we need them to do and goes a step further to explain why. Taking the time to explain the why is a huge step toward having influence and getting others to buy into our plan. In this case, the initiative of paying attention to details and being more inquisitive in the work environment is what we are striving to achieve. The why here is pretty clear and true in so many cases. Little things can make a big difference.

I recall John Wooden, the famous UCLA basketball coach and leader, teaching his players how to lace up their shoes. Lacing up shoes was just one of the many seemingly minor things that Wooden taught, but his success goes without question. And these minor things obviously made a big impact. Wooden was convinced that little things can make a big difference. I'm with Coach on that issue. I sure can't argue with his success.

Paying attention to key details and having a healthy inquisitive attitude can take an average operation to well above average. This type focus can make any organization, facility, team, or operation better! The real question is how can we lead our team to this level of engagement and thinking? The following are some ideas on leading this effort and moving our team member to be more inquisitive and ultimately toward a culture of ownership in the organization.

1. Narrow the focus again. While we have talked about narrowing the focus in organizational objectives and communication events, we need to also narrow the focus when we are talking about taking care of the details. We need to identify which details are critical to success. These are the items that we can't afford to compromise on to be successful. These are the items that have to be executed at a high level all the time for us to achieve our desired results. Once we have identified what may be seemingly small things that can make a big difference, we can then work on putting systems in place to ensure we execute those tasks consistently and effectively.

2. Go beyond "what" to "why." In our communication efforts, both broadly and individually, we need to always be sure we do more than just tell people what we want done. We also need to explain why it matters. The explanation of why would also need get back to why it matters to the group or individual as well. Make it personal. When you take the time to explain and teach why, you are influencing and taking on a very basic leadership role. Most people will more likely comply with a request from the manager or supervisor if they understand why it matters and why it is important. You may think that you shouldn't have to take this time because people should just do what you say without questioning, but let's be honest here. Are you interested in the so-called power of being the boss or having influence with your team to achieve more? Take the time and explain why. It will have a huge, lasting impact.

3. Break down the walls. Departmental walls hinder overall teamwork in the organization and limit the inquisitive nature of everyone involved. If we really want people to pay attention to details and be inquisitive about the operation, we must ensure everyone is aligned with the same

goals and objectives. The focus must be the same for everyone. Align everyone with the same overall objectives, break down departmental walls, and by all means, eliminate unhealthy competition in the facility. Sure, everyone and every department needs to do their part, but not at the expense of another department. Executing the details well takes everyone pulling in the same direction. I have witnessed too many examples over the years of managers pitting crews against one another in the spirit of healthy competition. I understand the competitive nature, but I prefer to have everyone pulling together to achieve as one group winning together. Trust me, you will know if someone or some group is not doing their part.

4. Inspect what you expect. If something is important, you need to make it a big deal and pay attention to it. If detail housekeeping around a machine center is key for safety, then you need to monitor it regularly and address issues timely. Sure, reinforce quality work when you see it, but correct subpar performance when you see it too. If you don't pay attention to what you communicate is important, then others won't pay attention either. If little things matter, then pay attention to the little things. If you want team members to be inquisitive about operating issues, then you ask questions and get them thinking. Leaders set the tone and drive the cultural focus for the entire team.

5. Recognize the care. Employees that are inquisitive are those that care. When you see employees paying attention to details and taking this type of initiative in the workplace, recognize it and make it a big deal. You want to reinforce the desired behavior, but you also want to influence future behavior. You are going to send a message either way when someone displays this type behavior. If you ignore it, you are sending a message that it really wasn't that big a deal. If you highlight it and recognize it, you reinforce what you are looking for from team members. Timely reinforcement impacts the individual or team involved as well as everyone

else aware of the situation. People are watching how the leader responds to all situations. Recognition is a powerful tool to drive attention to detail and an inquisitive focus in the workplace.

SUMMARY

It's not surprising that the successful implementation any desired behavior change in the workplace will come down to the effectiveness of leadership. Narrowing the focus, communicating the expectations, leading by example, and providing the necessary attention are all key steps in the process of driving the type of change we are talking about in this chapter. Those same steps are often true regarding any type of change management approach in an organization. Simplify everything you can, communicate well, and execute the basics brilliantly. If we want to move our people toward an ownership culture in the workplace, we need to realize owners take initiative and that we need to create an environment to facilitate that type of behavior. Leaders create that atmosphere!

THE REST OF THE STORY

We found great success in engaging our people to control that white board and flip chart. Their engagement level and attention to detail did increase with that focus effort. Our keys to the success were finding a systematic-type approach that could be sustained while we attempted to drive this culture change. Providing a simple approach for team members to both engage and to commit to the process were key factors in our achieving the desired results we wanted. The safety committee was a huge success, and they came back with some great ideas and input on some detail areas of the plant that made a sustained impact. One of the key items that came from this team working with our leadership team was a simplified advancement of our pre-task assessment approach for our maintenance personnel. This approach was really a pre-work assessment of the details associated with the job to be performed where we would have our team member simply ask two questions. What can injure me? How can I do this task safely? These two simple questions being evaluated and responded to on the work order ticket made a huge impact to our safety performance. We came up with an efficient approach for our maintenance personnel to get into the details and be more inquisitive in an area that was so important to our success and to our team member's safety. Safety for our people had to come first!

While working without a maintenance manager lasted about eighteen months, we were able to tear down a departmental wall that was a barrier to our culture change in this area during this time period. Once we filled the position, we made sure that we did not allow that wall to be reconstructed by our maintaining one set of objectives for the entire facility. All of our managers and supervisors had the same objectives to ensure we maintained complete alignment.

The benefits in this area of culture change were impactful. While the benefits weren't necessarily obvious on a daily basis, team members being more inquisitive and paying attention to details did make an impact over time. The routine attention to detail with team members being more inquisitive regarding their roles and challenging items that would have normally gone unaddressed were very key to the facility's success. We noticed improvements in all three areas (safety, quality, and productivity) that we targeted for our focus. In addition, we took another major step in moving our workforce toward a culture of ownership.

Key learnings:

1. Strategy and execution must work together to achieve success.
2. Little things done well over time can make a big difference. Do them well.
3. Pay attention to what matters. People are watching.
4. Go beyond the "what" to explain the "why."
5. Don't forget a narrow focus is always a good idea.

CHAPTER 9

OWNERS ARE INTEGRAL TO STAFFING NEEDS

My story

During the pandemic issues of 2020 and 2021, we experienced some severe staffing challenges in a couple of the facilities that I supported as a regional general manager. Initially these staffing shortages were the results of employees contracting the virus or coming into close contact with someone that was diagnosed with the illness. We found various ways to work through those type staffing-related shortages and did a great job of limiting the close contacts in the facilities with some pretty significant changes to how we operated our plants. We made changes to the way we accomplished work, provided breaks, held meetings, and conducted our business in a variety of ways.

However, the pandemic was just the start of staffing challenges in a few of these facilities. As pandemic issues started to decline, more businesses started to open back up, and the need for employees to rejoin the workforce became a real issue for some companies. While we never curtailed any operations as we were an essential industry, we started to see the pull on our workforce toward other opportunities in several key market areas of the country. Other businesses began to offer higher wages, sign-on bonuses, retention bonuses, and many other incentives to entice people to leave where they were working to join them. We quickly found ourselves in another staffing shortage in a few of our locations as we suffered some significant resignations in a fairly short period of time. Other companies used money to be the primary means to lure people from their current jobs to something different in these select markets.

I noticed similar issues occurring in regions all over the country as demand for workers drove some very high wage-rate offerings along with many of these special bonus payments. With these now urgent staffing challenges, I noticed some very creative approaches in recruiting by our people. Some of those were likely more successful than others, but there were some very creative approaches devised to attract new employees. My thoughts on this matter were not negative toward these approaches, but I wanted us to see this opportunity in a different light. If we have created a desirable place to work and have moved our employee base toward an ownership mentality with a real engagement focus, we should be able to look to our existing team members to be a key part of this solution. These people are an integral part of attracting and retaining newer employees. Engaged team members are the most effective communication means to the community and can be real ambassadors for our organization. These people are invested in the facility and can represent us in their various spheres of influence. I would much rather have a referral from an existing employee than take a chance on someone that we don't have any knowledge of other than through the interview process.

Elevating the view of our existing team members to integral parts of the staffing process also helps further move them along toward a cultural of ownership. This focus begins with them being an ambassador in their various communities, churches, recreational events, and anywhere they come in contact with people. People are going to talk about where they work with their friends and acquaintances, so we hope those discussions are positive and appealing to others when they talk about our facility or organization.

When we share our staffing needs with our team members and engage them in being part of the solution, we are furthering their ownership mentality in the facility. I really challenged our facilities to engage their folks in being part of this solution. While it was a new concept for some of them, it was not a hard approach to grasp. We merely need to share our needs with our team members, ask for their involvement, and direct them to how they can help in us both attracting and retaining employees. They could help us attract people by sharing our needs with people they know that would be a good fit for our organization. We just wanted them to consider people that they would enjoy working with and that would fit the culture that we were building. With respect to retaining people, we really needed to do a good job of on boarding, training, and making new people feel comfortable in our facility. We really needed to get new personnel to feel like part of the team as soon as possible.

Our existing workforce could be key to both aspects of these staffing needs. They could be great ambassadors in attracting new employees and a great benefit to our retention efforts as we moved people through the first ninety days of employment. People do care about who they work with and want to have adequate staffing to reduce their hours worked, so there is direct motivation for people to be engaged in this twofold effort of attracting and retaining. Our team members thus should be an integral part of our staffing efforts. So we move forward with engaging them in this effort.

A NEW LOOK AT STAFFING AND RETENTION

As we consider the challenges of attracting and retaining employees in today's work environment, we need to look at the culture in our workplace and our existing workforce to be the keys to long-term staffing success. The entire purpose of this book is to create a culture in our facilities and within our organizations that is desirable for people. In this chapter, we are specifically addressing the benefits of this ownership culture in staffing needs. When our team members become owners, they are an integral part of the answers to staffing issues. The following are some specific actions that you can take to create this type atmosphere for your team members to be an integral part of this process.

1. Culture beats strategy all day long. In prior chapters, we have discussed the importance and balance of strategy and execution. These are two essential elements to any business, athletic team, or any organization for that matter. However, culture is the most important factor when we talk about sustaining results, creating an environment that attracts people, and retaining our workforce. Create a culture that people want to be associated with as they enter the workforce. Engage those same people to both attract and retain employees to be a part of that culture. You need to seek to create the most desirable place to work in your market area. Yes, you will have to still be competitive with wages and benefits and may lose some people from time to time due to better opportunities for them; but in the long-term, culture will prevail, and you will have the staffing levels needed.

2. Community visibility matters. When seeking to hire or address any type of staffing needs in the facility, it always helps to have a strong presence in the community. People need to know you are there and need to know a little about your operation. Be involved with the local business organizations and participate in local events as much as possible. Support the community with your time, your money, and your talents. Ensure signage is sufficient to proclaim your presence and be sure your grounds are well maintained. Establish relationships with community leaders and other businesses in your area. Don't shy away from media attention when you can present a positive story about your business or something related to your people. Be as visible as you can in your community and sphere of influence. Highlight your team members every chance you get.

3. Team members can be ambassadors. If we have solid culture of engagement and our team members have a posi-

tive view of the workplace, these team members can be our most effective ambassadors in the community for attracting new employees. The great thing here is that they can tell our story; and we don't spend valuable resources (money or time) on advertising, hiring events, or other candidate seeking endeavors. Our people can really be an integral part of our staffing process if we have the right internal environment. We need to inform them of the need and equip them with some information to be effective in their respective spheres of influence outside the workplace. Think of each team member as a walking advertisement when they leave the facility. Ask yourself this question though. What is that advertisement saying about our operation?

4. Trainers and mentors matter. Take some time and evaluate your training program for new employees. I have seen far too many instances of new people just being put into a room to watch endless hours of training video. Sure, use the videos to assist in this onboarding process, but interact with your people regularly and get them out into the work environment soon and often. Break up those video sessions with some hands-on learning too. Select trainers that enjoy teaching others, have communication skills, and are patient with new employees. Don't just send people to work where the openings are in the facility. Not all of our team members are geared to be good with new people. Not all experienced operators are good trainers.

    Also, consider a mentor program in addition to just skills training on the job. I bet you have some more senior people that would enjoy mentoring new employees. This mentorship approach just provides another layer of investing in our new people to help retain them in that challenging first few months of employment. Many companies lose far too many people in the ninety days of employment because we don't take the time to ensure the on boarding and training process is meeting the needs of the new hire. A mentorship program during this time period could be the answer and alleviate much of this problem. In summary, develop an approach to enable your team members to be an integral part of this onboarding process.

5. Engage broadly. When we think of engagement, we often think of the internal manner of leading and valuing our people. In this case, build on that thought and think beyond just our existing team members at work. Consider holding open house events where people in the community can tour our facility (be safe and limit access where needed) and learn more about our operation. Allow team members to show family members what they do every day at work. People like talking about what they do and really enjoy showing family members their skills. Also consider visible events in the community like family day picnics where employees can connect with each other outside of work. These types of events further strengthen the bond of a workforce and engage at a deeper level. Team members will want to tell others about their work experience and be more integral in the staffing needs of the organization.

SUMMARY

If you are having trouble attracting new employees or retaining people, I would take an honest assessment of your workplace culture before I went and spent a lot of money or time advertising and recruiting. If your current workforce is disengaged, it will be a challenge to hire and retain regardless of what you do. Work on that culture so that your existing team members can be an integral part of the solution and be those ambassadors in the community that you need representing your organization. As you move your organization to one of an ownership culture, you will find your team members to be that integral part of the staffing and retention process to help you through those challenging times.

THE REST OF THE STORY

Staffing issues across the region looked very different depending on which facility we focused on. A few that were less developed with respect to an ownership culture and that were in a more competitive market faced more serious challenges. Those with more established cultures and in less competitive job markets had fewer challenges to deal with in staffing. We attacked these challenges in the same manner though regardless of the situation. We focused on creating better workplaces to solidify the base and made various changes to work schedules, trying to create more time off for our people. Time off was probably the second largest issue to deal with after wage rates. People wanted weekends off, and they made it very clear that was a key issue.

To address these concerns, we adjusted shift schedules and actually walked away from some business to lighten the customer order load on the facilities. While reducing our customer load was a difficult decision to act on, that reduction played a major role in controlling those weekend overtime hours. We also made a point to rotate weekend work whenever we could to allow for more team members to have time off. Time off was a major issue with our team members, and we had to make adjustments to meet their needs. Listening to our team members was very key during this time period!

In addition, while we weren't competing to have the highest wage offering in our market areas, we knew that we had to be competitive to degree. We did some market survey and analysis to make some very targeted wage adjustments in a few areas. We participated to a degree with sign-on bonus and referral bonus offerings. These were not our primary focuses though for attracting and retaining employees, but rather just an attempt to not lose at this stage. The key was to be competitive in wages but not try to keep up with everyone in the respective markets. Our real focus was to create desirable places to work long-term and let that be our mantra.

We saw immediate success in some areas, with others taking a little longer to make progress due to the inherent challenges we encountered. Through all of these efforts, I was very pleased with not only the staffing progress but the operational results of many of these facilities during these challenging times. It was obvious that our focus on culture and creating a desirable workplace was paying off. The focus was not complete by any means, but the process and foundation were in place to yield favorable results going forward.

We noted benefits in modifying the onboarding process to engage the employees on the floor sooner and more often in their first few weeks. Needless to say, the onboarding process changes we made were effective. We had a great online tool, but we used that tool to complement on-the-floor experience and exposure to our people. We also selected trainers to perform the actual hands-on skills training on the manufacturing floor. We need team members that were skilled and wanted to teach new employees. Never again would we just place new employees with just anyone for this very key process.

We were also effective in establishing mentor programs in numerous facilities that provided major benefits in the retention focus during the first ninety days of employment. This mentor program provided an effective approach to keep our new employees close to a more senior employee that was interested helping new folks assimilate into the workplace. The mentors were all volunteers and just possessed a desire to help others feel comfortable in a new environment. The mentor program was really just ensuring new people had someone to go to with questions or issues.

All of these focused areas were instrumental in hiring, retaining, and furthering the engagement level of our team. Getting team members to be an integral part of the process was the key. Once we were successful in tapping into a very key resource for addressing staffing needs, we were able to more effectively meet these new challenges. Not only did we meet the challenges, we were able to move our team members further along in the ownership culture focus.

Key learnings:

1. Don't run a sweat shop and be surprised that you have staffing issues.
2. Create a desirable place to work and allow your team members to be ambassadors for you.

3. The organization needs to be visible in the community.
4. Develop a training and mentor plan that utilizes the right people.

CHAPTER 10

OWNERS INVEST

My story

Going back to that first general manager assignment back in the early 1990s, I realized a few years into that assignment that we needed everyone to be invested in our operation beyond the typical employee-and-employer relationship. As we were moving our team members toward an ownership mentality that would change the culture of our organization, we knew we would have to create an opportunity for our people to invest in the operation if we really wanted to drive this ownership concept to its full extent. The investing would obviously not be a financial investment that an owner would normally make in purchasing a tangible piece of property but rather a different kind of investment. Our team members needed to invest themselves to a deeper level of caring and engagement in our operation. While we had briefly touched on this concept in the new identity phase, we need to reexplore this concept and go deeper with it to further our culture change. If we could achieve that goal, we would definitely continue to move our team members toward a culture of ownership.

To achieve this goal, we targeted our focus on two primary needs in the facility for a dual purpose. We wanted to provide the structure for this investment opportunity to focus on enhancing our key customer relationships and improving our machine reliability. Those two key areas are vitally important for any manufacturing organization. Taking care of customers and taking care of machines are the lifeblood to any industrial manufacturing business. With that framework in mind, we initiated the champion program. Specifically, we initiated a customer champion program and a machine champion program. The two champion programs would provide us a framework to drive investment opportunities for key personnel, as well as target improvement efforts in two very key areas of our operation.

The customer champion program was aimed at selecting an operating employee from the production floor to serve as the champion for one of our top customers. We focused initially on our top ten accounts with this approach. We selected ten individuals that would be matched with one of these ten accounts. Ideally, the individuals selected would be directly involved with the manufacturing of the customer's product in some capacity or would have some direct involvement with serving the respective customer that they were matched with in this program. The champion would make an initial visit to the customer location with our technical sales representative that was assigned to the account. The program did not change the role of the technical service representative nor the customer service representative assigned to the account. The champion was merely and additional resource to allow us to better service the account through an increased awareness of customer needs and issues. These needs and issues would now be known firsthand by those most impactful to meeting those needs and resolving those issues. The customer champion would make monthly contact either through visiting the customer or participating on a conference call with the other personnel assigned to the account.

The twofold goal with this customer champion program was to increase the customer focus on the manufacturing floor but also to increase the ownership focus of our team members. The champions would be investing more of themselves in this effort and taking more of a personal ownership role with respect to the key issues associated with the accounts selected for this program. The champion focus would also serve our organization well during customer visits as our champions could be very involved in those visits and discussions.

The second major focus area was reliability. We initiated a similar program that we referred to as our machine champion program. We assigned each of our maintenance team members to a specific manufacturing machine. They were named the machine champions for those respective machines. Machine champions were not relieved of other duties nor did they focus all of their attention to just their assigned machine but rather took the lead on preventative maintenance planning and execution for their machine, interacted frequently with machine operators to ensure work orders were in the system for key concerns, and spent discretionary maintenance time on their machines working with crews to improve overall reliability results in a number of ways. We were looking for a way to improve reliability, to move our maintenance team toward a reliability focus, and to grow the ownership focus with those technicians. We were able to do all of those things by creating an approach that provided an investment opportunity for the team members.

While these champion programs would be the basis for our investing focus in the facility, we also looked for specific events to aid in getting more people to invest as well. Major events that employees can be a part of can help drive this investment component as well. Major initiatives like the move toward a 5S program for plant organization can really drive employee ownership and personal investment if the team members are allowed to be involved in every stage of the process and share the accountability for the sustained success. We took advantage of these opportunities as much as possible to achieve this goal of giving our people an opportunity to invest and move them toward ownership.

CREATING OPPORTUNITIES TO INVEST

As you consider ways to drive investment opportunities in your organization, take advantage of the dual needs and goals as I mentioned above. There is nothing wrong with achieving multiple goals with one action. We avoid additional projects or distractions when we implement initiatives that are woven into the daily work process. This type of approach is much easier for managers and supervisors to lead and ensure results are actually accomplished. In addition, the more we can engage our people in things that are key to business success, the better work environment we can create for everyone involved. Always think of engagement as a tool to drive results and not a separate human resource initiative that just creates more work for the leadership team. Integrate these initiatives into the normal business focus of your operation. You will be more successful and save yourself a great deal of time if we have a cohesive approach, focusing on normal business operations, as opposed to administrative initiatives that are not aligned with operational focus.

The following are some general ideas to help facilitate a framework to allow your team members to invest in the operation and allow your organization to move toward a culture of ownership:

1. Keep the main things the main thing. As you look for opportunities for your people to invest, stay focused on key business needs and avoid just creating excess work. Find dual goal opportunities when you can, and save yourself some time. By staying focused and developing initiatives aimed at driving these narrowly focused results, we are able to keep our workforce paying attention to what really matters. Anything you can do to provide people a deeper opportunity to contribute to these main things provides your team members a chance to invest in the organization and also to invest in themselves.

2. Investment requires sacrifice. While we aren't sacrificing personal financial resources in the workplace scenario, we still need sacrifice to generate a real investment. People invest here through sacrificing discretionary time, effort, commitment, or any other actions that lead them to drive a stake in some aspect of the operation to signify their investment. The key with this objective is that investment needs to be something that can be seen or observed by others. That observation can be a customer relationship, a physical area of the facility, or a visible outcome of a task that must

be completed! The key is here that the team member has to give something of themselves to move toward ownership.

3. Investment does require ability. Just like engaging in a financial transaction for a tangible piece of property requires the investor to have the means to make the investment, we have to ensure our team members have the ability and means to be successful within our framework as well. We would not assign someone to invest in being a customer champion that was weak in communicating or had shown little desire for serving others. Rather, we would look for individuals that were eager to engage, were organized on follow up initiatives, and would communicate well with other employees to broaden everyone's understanding of the customer's needs or issues. Team members without such skills could invest in other ways. Know your team and ensure you create opportunities conducive to your team member's skillsets.

4. Investments can take time to provide benefits. Don't rush things when creating opportunities for your people to invest. Start small and let things grow and mature over time. Investments can take time before you realize the benefits. The more time that team members are engaged in a process that helps them to drive their stake in the ground, the more likely they are to make a fully engaged investment and move toward an ownership mentality. Don't give up on the process if you don't see benefits right away. Create an investment-focused environment using targeted programs where appropriate, and allow your team members to invest on a regular basis.

SUMMARY

Whether you are in the early stages of driving culture change, in the midst of that initiative, or just putting the final touches on full implementation, you will find that this investment concept is a key piece to moving others toward ownership. Owners need to invest, and we need to find ways to help them make those investments. Leaders remove obstacles and provide opportunities for others to be successful. Helping our team members invest is a place to provide those opportunities! Take a look at your business and see where your team members can start making investments.

THE REST OF THE STORY

In summary, we had great success with both of the champion programs. The customer champion program was well received by our customers, and we even targeted expansion beyond just the initial top ten accounts. This added customer focus was helpful in the facility and really set us apart from our competitors in the market. Most importantly, it really drove investment and ownership with some of our team members. We did also see operational benefits as key quality issues were addressed more timely, and those unique requests that certain customers had were fulfilled more effectively.

The machine champion program was equally as successful. We saw reliability improvements and key operating metrics improve, but again, the key was that we also saw investment and ownership take place by our maintenance department. That program made a big impact on moving us from a maintenance identity for those folks (repair things) to a reliability identity (keep things running). These team members made a personal investment and took ownership.

There were other events that we took advantage of during that time period to drive investment and ownership with other employees too. We just had to remember to get people involved in planning stages, the execution phase, and the evaluation phase of any major project or program initiative to ensure we got the full benefit of the investment concept.

All things considered, we were successful in creating these opportunities for team members to invest and move toward ownership. Some of the people responded quickly while others took a little longer to engage. Regardless, the benefits were noticeable, and the overall engagement levels were improved. Our intentional efforts of creating opportunities for our team members to invest really enhanced our cultural of ownership in the workplace. The operating and commercial results also improved!

Key learnings:

1. Investment requires sacrifice. Create an atmosphere where team members can invest!
2. Elevating one's role and providing personal responsibility can create investment.
3. Keep the main thing the main thing.
4. Investment requires ability and may take time. Equip team members and be patient.

CHAPTER 11

LEADERS ARE INSIDE OUT

For the past seven chapters, I have outlined the *Is* to ownership and essentially the Is to teamwork. Who said there was no I in team? With that framework and content now established, I need to share one other very key I with you, and that's the word *inside*. Effective leaders are driven from a strong set of internal convictions and a purpose focused on people. This internal focus is the force behind what we see on the outside. Thus, leaders always work from the inside to the outside (inside out). The actions we see, communications we hear, and visions we follow are all a result of what's inside the leader. We often judge the effectiveness of a leader based on what we see or hear from them. However, to truly know the motivations behind the actions or comments, we have to know the heart of a leader.

What's on the inside will eventually surface over time. The inner convictions of a leader will be revealed the longer one is in a position of authority and deals with people. The frequency of interactions, the number of decisions made, and the sheer time with people will ultimately reveal one's character. In addition, a moment of crisis may speed that revelation up quite a bit. There's nothing more character revealing for a leader than how one reacts in a challenging moment. It's in these moments that conviction, character, and overall leadership skills are brought to the surface. I often use the analogy of a cup of liquid. You may see the cup is full from a distance but not know exactly what is inside the cup. However, if that cup gets bumped, whatever is on the inside will spill out. I sure hope when I get bumped that I'm comfortable with what spills out of me. Short of time or crisis, we just have to probe a little to really understand what's going on inside a leader. The conviction on the inside will set the tone for what we eventually see on the outside.

With that factor in mind, those of us desiring to lead others need to make an honest assessment of ourselves as leaders. Do we really want what's best for those team members that we aspire to lead? Are we willing to sacrifice personal gain for the betterment of those we lead? Do we genuinely care about the long-term well-being of those we are leading? Those are all questions that we need to be comfortable answering to truly know what's going on inside of us as leaders. We need to know those answers before we start taking action. As I said earlier, what's on the inside will eventually come out for others to see. Sometimes it takes that crisis to reveal the real character of a leader, but it will eventually be revealed. It's during those crisis times that our followers need us the most!

Over the last few years, I have seen my share of crises and challenging situations. I have seen various reactions from people in managerial roles and positions that provide opportunities for expanded leadership influence. I have witnessed selfless acts of leaders putting follower's needs ahead of business results, and yet I have also witnessed selfish acts placing more burden on team members. Tough times can bring out the best or worst in a leader. A leader therefore needs a strong set of core values to guide them through challenging times to ensure we maintain that follower-first focus.

I say all of that because making the culture changes that have been discussed in the prior chapters will require real leadership. This type of a leader is someone that will engage in the process's steps to culture change noted in chapter 3. This type of leader understands the long-term focus of business and doesn't get caught up in short term, finite games. This type of leader has a genuine desire to create a better workplace for their people regardless of whether the results improve or not (although I bet they do improve). This type of leader will sacrifice to ensure the environment is better for those they are leading. We may not see many examples of this type of leadership in our society today, but the need is as great as it has ever been. There has never been a time when effective leaders weren't needed. The present time is no exception. Whether we are talking about leading a transformational culture change in an organization, leading a governmental institution, leading a nonprofit organization, or leading a family, we need solid leadership today.

If you have this genuine desire on the inside and want to drive culture change in your organization, there are some basic concepts that you can follow to aid in your efforts. These concepts are more general in nature and could be applied to various change initiatives, but they do relate well to changing culture. I have found these to be helpful over the years in changing culture, driving change, and merely just investing in people. As you consider your next steps in culture change of any magnitude, consider the following concepts before you take action.

1. It all starts with purpose. As you get beyond the cliché vision and mission statements circulating around organizations today and get serious about real purpose, don't settle for a results-based purpose. Results are what you want to accomplish, and those are important. I concede that we had better deliver results to stay impactful in our roles, but that's not our purpose. Real, sustainable purpose though is who focused. That who for you could be your followers, your customers, people in the community, people served by your organization, or any number of potential whos. As I said, don't get me wrong, the whats and results do matter, but that's not purpose. Purpose is who-based and needs to be at the center of your focus as you look to change culture.

2. Communicate a clear vision, and don't compromise. Be clear on your expectations when you are looking to make changes and don't compromise on these items. People need to clearly understand what's changing, why it's changing, and not get confused by inconsistent leadership. Identify those key items that we are going to move forward with as the basis of our change, and never allow anyone to compro-

mise adherence to these items. If these items are important to making change work, then they are important all the time. Don't confuse your people by compromising key elements of the proposed system when challenges arise. Stay the course.

3. What we talk about most matters. Needless to say, people talk about what matters most to them. Family, hobbies, successes, struggles, etc., are all examples of things people will talk about most. It's no different in the workplace. What we talk about most will be viewed as the most important things by our followers. If we want to drive sustaining change, talk about what matters most in that process. Ask questions to followers related to those topics. Place the focus of your meetings on these key topics. Talk about those topics during informal conversations. Provide visual communication for those topics. The leader needs to practice great discipline here in conversation, announcements, and topics covered in meetings. What the leader focuses on most will be viewed by team members as the most important things!

4. Consistency is key. A consistent message coupled with consistent actions on behalf of the leader ensures a clear message is conveyed to the followers. I can't stress enough the importance of consistency in instituting change. There will be challenges along the way and temptations to forgo initiatives when the organization confronts obstacles. When your team or organization runs into a challenge and you start to feel pressure all around you, you will be tempted to fold up the tents and go home. You will be tempted to go back to the old ways and work your way through the difficulty. When you forgo the focus of culture change and elevate other priorities (devaluing people in many cases), you are sending a strong message to your team whether you speak a word or not. Trust me, people are watching to see just how serious we are about change when confronted with an unexpected challenge. Maintaining focus

and having the discipline to stay the course will go a long way to getting your team on board with the change. Keep that long-term focus and always go back to purpose when facing challenges. Your purpose should be your grounding force whenever things get unsettled, and you need to stabilize your team and yourself. Purpose matters. So be sure you have a solid one identified.

Those four concepts are really true for any change management approach, but in the area of culture change, they are very relevant. As we seek to move our team from a renter mentality to one of an owner, we will need to be skilled in the area of change management. Some organizations will require more change than others, but very few have a true culture of ownership. Those organizations with a strong engagement level may be closer to this ownership mentality but likely have some work to do as well. Others that have not addressed the engagement concept in their environment will have a much more significant change to make. We are really talking about taking engagement to a very high level with this ownership-culture approach. It's like taking the next step past an engagement type focus in the workplace. An ownership mentality in the workplace is pretty high-level engagement!

More than anything though, culture change takes leadership. Leadership is about influence, and that's what we are doing when we take a workforce through a culture-change process. Leaders that are fully committed to their team members position themselves to be the most successful in this change process. I agree with the concept that everything rests and falls on the quality of the leadership. If we want a workplace culture of owners and the benefits that result from that culture, then we need to provide outstanding leadership in the transformation process. This outstanding leadership starts in the inside of a leader and works its way out.

Key learnings:

1. Internal motivations eventually surface.
2. Purpose matters and needs to focus on who and not what.

3.   What we talk about most matters most.
4.   Maintain consistency of the message, and don't compromise.
5.   Change requires leadership.

95

CHAPTER 12

LOOKING BACK TO LOOK AHEAD

My story

As I look back over a thirty-plus-year career in business, I have seen more facilities than I can count, encountered more challenges than I could have imagined, and experienced results on every end of the spectrum. With all that said though, what I remember most are the people that I was fortunate enough to work with during these years. To be honest, I don't remember too many specific financial results or operational milestones, but I can still picture the faces of people from that first assignment to the last one. There were so many people in so many different locations. There are a few things they all had in common regardless of their position, pay scale, location, or union affiliation. Everyone wanted to go home safely each day. Everyone needed the job to take care of financial obligations. Lastly, everyone desired a place to work where they were cared about beyond their work, valued as a person, and treated with respect. I noticed those basic desires from people early on and found them to be unchanged through the years regardless of location or the business climate.

During this same time period, I had the opportunity to witness many examples of management and leadership. I define *management* as getting work done through others and *leadership* as influence. I maintain they are two different elements of directing people. With that in mind, I saw many different styles and approaches to managing and to leading others. To be honest, I saw some great examples and some that were pretty bad. I saw some examples of leadership that really had people's best interest in mind and some examples that may have never given consideration to their people's needs at all. Through all of these experiences, I have come away with a sincere desire to make the workplace better. I don't want to make it less efficient, more costly, less competitive, or anything of that nature. I'm a degreed accountant, worked as a CPA, and managed businesses for over thirty years. I clearly understand what it takes to operate a financially sound business. I am not diminishing the financial needs of a business nor the challenges. I merely want to create workplace environments that can achieve financial success and still be a desirable place to work. I want places of work where people are cared about regardless of their position and valued for who they are in addition to what they do. These places would challenge team members, have a high degree of accountability, and yet operate more like a family than a prototypical business. These places would be operations where people look out for one another and not step on one another. These places would allow for people to do their best work every day and progress to reach their potential. These places would obviously need sound leaders!

Work-life balance would be less an issue if our workplaces were more desirable places to earn a living. Don't get me wrong, work is going to be hard and challenging. Those are the reasons we get paid to do it, but the workplace doesn't have to be a cold, callous environment. Leaders set the tone for the workplace. Leaders shape and build the culture. In the preceding chapters, I have provided some very specific actionable items to move your organization from a renter mentality to one of an owner mentality. I have based those concepts on actual experiences that I have implemented over my career. Each of them contributed in some way to creating a culture in the workplace that people found more desirable. Furthermore, the continued investment in leaders to continue to drive and sustain this culture was a key factor in the success. Culture change requires leaders that are willing to commit to the process over a period of time. Not only are these leaders committed to the process, but they also must be committed to their people. Yes, everything does begin and end with leadership.

I hope you feel as committed to this process of improving the workplace as I do. After thirty-plus years in business, I want to share those experiences to create value, provide a vision of a better environment, and truly make people's lives better. There are numerous ways to add value to people and to be impactful in their lives. I have simply chosen the workplace as my target area to achieve those purposes. The workplace is often written about, but seldom from the employee's perspective. I want to equip leaders to create that better environment and have that positive impact.

The next section is a summary of key questions to give consideration to in regard to embarking on culture change. These series of questions are essentially the playbook to move forward.

THE PLAYBOOK TO MOVE FORWARD
5 W's AND AN H

Why: why should we commit to moving our team members to an ownership culture in the workplace?

1. It is the right thing to do for our people.

    Fundamentally, it sure just seems like caring for people and valuing people for who they are and not just what they do makes sense. At the heart of the issue is the leader's concern for the people. We should want to create a desirable place to work, and the truth of the matter is that we can both create that culture and be financially successful. We don't have to trade one for the other. Our people can help drive that success if provided an atmosphere and culture to participate in the process. So often, we just relegate people to a task and call it a job. What I am proposing here is that while those tasks still have to be accomplished, we do so with a different perspective and mindset. We care about our team members, value these team members, and provide an opportunity for them to be engaged and contribute beyond just completing an assignment. After all, that's how we would want to be treated. It is just the right thing to do for many reasons.

2.   It will improve staffing and retention issues.

Let's face it, creating a desirable place to work is not at the top of many executives' priority list these days. Leaders that will commit to this vision will see benefits in both attracting and retaining employees. At some point, the wage battle will settle out and the real winners in the staffing area will be those that provide a desirable place to work. People want to be in an environment where they feel safe, secure, wanted, and have an ability to express themselves in a number of ways. Engagement is more than a human resource topic of discussion. It is a real lever to attract people, retain people, and drive business results. As we have seen in recent months, staffing issues can cripple a business, a supply chain, and a nation. We need people, and these people need to be engaged in their work. Moving toward a culture of ownership is the ultimate engagement focus.

3.   Increased engagement will improve operating and financial results.

While I have already stated that moving to a culture of ownership and driving engagement is the right thing to do regardless of results, it is obvious that having complete alignment and everyone working as one team produces improved results. Increased focus, care, and discretionary effort are all components of this ownership culture. An increased focus on each other, toward our customers, and on process reliability are all derived from this level of engagement. While a leader won't use all the opinions and ideas provided by the team members, there will be many that will be helpful over the course of time. Increased engagement levels will improve all facets of the operation. How could it not?

When: when should a leader undertake a move to an ownership culture?

1. The organization is suffering from low morale, staffing issues, and/or poor results.

    If you are experiencing any of these challenges, give consideration to this culture change. As you have read, this ownership culture addresses each of these issues to varying degrees and may be just what your organization needs to overcome the challenges. While I would recommend not waiting until you are deep in the midst of a staffing struggle to implement such culture change, it is possible to start at any point or level in the process. If you are struggling for answers, give consideration to how investing in your people may be the key to climbing out of the valley.

2. The organization has plateaued on engagement and needs new energy.

    If you have been focused on engagement for a while and feel you have plateaued, give consideration to taking the next step in engagement by going fully toward an ownership culture. If you have that solid baseline of engagement established, you will find the process just the next step in a natural progression. The ownership culture is what I would describe as the ultimate engagement focus for an organization. It may be time for that next step.

3. The leader wants to create a desirable work environment for people and leave a legacy.

    Like me, maybe you just have that desire to make a difference and be impactful with those you lead. Regardless of business conditions, employee engagement level, or any other circumstances surrounding your organization, you just want to make an impact. If you genuinely care about your followers and are looking for a way to add value to their lives, this culture change may be just what you are looking to implement and just what your team members need. When is it ever a bad time to create a more desirable place to work for our people?

Who: who do you need to undertake a transformation to an ownership culture?

1. Key leaders from the management team that are fully committed and have credibility with team members.

   Before you can take any major step with operating personnel, you have to get your key management team personnel on board. You need key leaders to be completely on board with you. If you have some that are not totally sold on the idea, you just have to make sure they are not actively working against you. While it is understandable to have some skeptics on a management team when talking about a change this significant, you can't proceed very long if some of the management team members are actively working against you. You have to deal with that issue. Again, while it's okay for some to take a wait-and-see approach, it is not okay to have key members working against you. Those obstructions have to be removed. The more key management team members that will commit to being leaders and leading this effort, the more successful you will be in the implementation phase.

2. Frontline leaders that are supportive.

   After you have key leaders at the management team level on board and resolved any major roadblocks with that team, frontline level leaders have to be the next focus. In reality, frontline leaders are where it really happens. Real engagement takes place at the frontline leader or supervisory level depending on how your organization is structured. We can talk all we want at the executive or management level, but execution is carried out at the frontline leader level. And this level will ultimately determine success of the initiative. Take the time to explain the benefits to the frontline leader and why they should be supportive.

Sell them on the why before telling them what you need them to do. Get their hearts engaged before their minds. You must have their support to be successful in changing culture. If you don't want this culture change to be just another good idea conceived in a board room that went nowhere, get the frontline leaders on board!

3. Team members that want a desirable workplace.

    Once you get key management leaders on board and frontline leaders engaged, you will turn your attention to your general workforce as a whole. Depending on your situation and current engagement level, you will get a range of responses. Some of the team members will likely embrace the concepts quickly, and some will take a wait-and-see approach. You will likely encounter some that will be very negative, but don't let that discourage you in any way. There will always be opposition to anything that is worthwhile. The opposition could be from a fear of change to just a plain old nasty attitude. It doesn't matter. If you fundamentally believe a culture change is what your organization needs, then you press on and move forward.

    Remember to sell the why before the what. If you invest time on the front end of communicating why it should matter to everyone and focus on the benefits to the team members, it will pay off. The key message is creating a better workplace for our people. The improved results are a secondary benefit. Don't get those out of order when talking with your team members. Be clear that the team members are the focus here.

What: what are the short and long-term expectations of moving toward an ownership culture?

1. Minor improvements that increase as new Is are added.

    Changing culture is sort of like starting a work out regiment. You get started on day one, put forth a great deal of effort, get sore, and see no results. Day two produced much the same thing. You think you are wasting your time and energy, but if you will just keep pushing forward, you will begin to see minor improvements. It will happen. When you see improvements starting to plateau, you introduce another element to the effort much like you would in a workout. This new element may create soreness again, but after several days, you will see the benefits. The key is consistency and commitment. You can't do it in a day or two, but over time, it will pay off. You don't get into shape after one or two workouts, but over time, you will see results. One workout on its own is really just a waste of time. However, a workout done day after day will make a huge difference. Culture change is the same way. If you want a culture of ownership in your workplace, then work at it every day. It will happen.

2. Turnover decreases and applicants increase as people want to be a part of the organization.

    As we create more desirable places to work, it is inevitable that we will retain more of our current employees and attract more of the kind of employees that will be a fit for our organization. Employees generally start looking for opportunities when they are dissatisfied with their current job for any number of reasons. If we can move our workplace to a culture of ownership, our team members will be more satisfied and content. We will likely see fewer of our team members seeking out or listening to other opportunities. Furthermore, with a highly engaged workforce and a cultural of ownership, we will quickly gain a solid reputation in the communities we operate in and have people wanting to join the team. So we both retain existing team members at a higher level and attract more candidates with this same focused effort of culture change! The reputation will continue to spread over time, and the results will be sustainable. Staffing issues should not be a problem once the ownership culture is fully ingrained in the workplace.

3. KPMs trend in positive direction as team members are aligned toward fewer goals.

    As we narrow our focus to only those key drivers that will ultimately determine the success of our operation, it will be easier to share this focus with all team members. As true KPMs are narrowed down to the three to five essentials to success, communication and tracking become much simpler to implement. A narrowed focus is the first step to streamlined actions for our team members too. This type of business focus goes hand in hand with a culture change to ownership. The more we can eliminate complexity and simplify the operation, the more we can share in the overall decision-making and ownership of the operation. With refinement in focus and progress on engagement, KPMs will inevitably be more prone to move in the right direction. Simplification, focus, and energy are the key drivers here. The more people we have pushing for the same things, the more likely we are to succeed. It's a sheer matter of more force pushing fewer things. Physics would say increased force pushing decreased matter will be much more likely to generate movement. The same methodology plays out here.

Where: where does the leader start to implement this transformation to a culture of ownership?

1. The leader's first move is an internal assessment.

    The first actionable step in changing culture is to pause and perform an internal self-assessment of one's organization. A leader needs to understand where the organization is currently with respect to engagement and how much credibility the leadership team has established with the workforce. In addition, the leader needs to gain a clear understanding of the position that key managers and front-line leaders have with respect to the culture change initiative. An honest self-assessment will enable the leader to fully grasp the key challenges that will be faced early on in the process and provide clarity as to how much time needs to be spent in the preparation phase before communicating with the workforce. The key is not to rush at this stage but rather take the time, ask hard questions, and talk to key managers and frontline leaders.

2. The management team has to be on board with key leaders willing to support the effort.

As with any major initiative, key managers have to be on board with any major initiative and be willing to step out of their managerial roles and be key leaders too. The organizational leader can do it alone in some cases depending on the size and structure of the organization, but the leader can't be fighting major opposition in the process. Several key managers can remain neutral, but they can't be openly opposed for the initiative to be successful. Total alignment and enthusiasm would be ideal, but that's not always possible. Here again, don't rush this process but rather spend time with key personnel explaining the concept, the benefits, and the process. Listen to concerns and clarify the vision to ensure communication is clear, concise, and presents the ultimate picture you envision of the workplace. If you have already invested in these relationships, you have likely already built credibility and will have success getting these people on board.

3. Address any negative managers and supervisors.

As noted earlier, some neutral parties are okay, but actively negative key managers or supervisors will undermine the effort. If you encounter those individuals, do your best to understand where the negativism is coming from, and the reason for the negative response to the initiative. If it is just a lack of understanding, take additional time and go deeper with the explanation. However, if it is just a lack of interest in creating a better workplace for our people or a general disinterest in advancing engagement, there may be a fundamental issue here that is problematic.

If you have a core value of caring for your people and want to lead them well at all levels of the organization, you must have all managers and supervisors committed to that same value. Maybe they aren't as focused on this value as you are, but they need to be invested to some degree.

While we may see various personnel express that commitment in different ways, we need to ensure that the core value is in fact accepted by our key managers and front-line leaders. These personnel are an extension of the facility leader, and while unique in some ways, must still exhibit the values of the organization to be a fit for the organization. If the core value and fit issues can't be resolved in a reasonable amount of time, you need to have some open discussions with those personnel. Chances are that they are not very happy in their role anyway if they see a set of core values that they can't buy into being established and a culture movement on the horizon that they can't get excited about being a part in leading. You need to have those tough discussions and resolve the matter before you get too far into the process. Many times, it will resolve itself over time, but don't ignore it nor wait too long.

How: how do we efficiently and effectively transform the culture to an ownership mentality?

1. Communicate the vision and why it should matter to everyone.

    Now that we have all the groundwork in place, it is time to communicate to the workforce. Anytime you communicate vision, start from where you are today. Establish the present reality for everyone in the room listening to your message. Talk briefly about the pros and cons of that present reality. Talk about the successes achieved and the challenges that still lie ahead. Share your desire to create a better workplace for your team members. Talk honestly about why that is important to you and what you mean by a better workplace. I would also suggest sharing that this better workplace can also lead to improved results which benefits everyone in a number of ways, including job security. Provide a brief vision of what you want to move toward with this culture change to an ownership mentality. Don't overwhelm the audience with too much information but rather just enough information to make the message appealing. Share with them just the initial steps and ensure it sounds simple yet appealing for them to engage at the appropriate time. Reemphasizing this change is directly geared to creating a more desirable workplace and one that truly engages everyone to be their best! As you close, acknowledge that you will need them for the transformation to be successful. Everyone plays a role!

2. Establish the owners' new identity (first I).

   After that initial communication, the leader needs to first establish that new identity in the team members. We have to provide leadership to help our team members start to see themselves differently before they will in turn act differently. The team members need to see themselves as owners before they will behave like owners. We start by just using different terminology. We now have team members, not employees. New team members join our team as opposed to get hired by our company. Where appropriate, we have joint leadership meetings with union leaders to discuss key topics and focus on what's best for our team members in this joint discussion. We really focus on building trust, mutual respect, and furthering credibility at this stage. We invest time with our people by asking questions, getting their opinions on matters, and elevating their view of themselves in the organization. We always need to go beyond just telling team members what needs to be done and take the time to explain why it matters or why it is important. As we elevate the identity of our team members, it is key that we lead well and not just manage and supervise. Leaders take the opportunity to have influence and going beyond what to why is a major step in this leadership focus. We must establish that new identity before we can move forward with the next steps in the cultural change initiative.

3. Provide the owners access to information (second I).

Now that we have established a new identity with our team members, it's time for us to provide access to information. The first step of identity establishment was a direct investment in our team members. Now we are going to open things up and provide access to key information to both inform them of matters relevant to them and outwardly display that we are serious about this culture change. The key with this step is to narrow the focus down to a few valuable topics or metrics that would be meaningful and helpful to the team members. Generally speaking, a workforce will always want to know what's important, how we are doing, and how they can help. As you narrow the focus down here, keep those three questions in mind.

Secondly, give some thought to the best way to communicate the information. Is it verbal, written, or a graphic-focused communication? I would always suggest a combination of these methods in some manner to provide various approaches and repetition in the communication effort. Keep in mind that less is more here. Keep it simple and consistent particularly in the early stages. You want team members to have a clear picture of what is important and drives the success of our business. You want those same team members to know exactly how we are performing and most importantly, how they can help us improve. I can't stress enough narrowing your business focus and simplifying the message here.

Beyond those key messages, be prepared to share other things that come up from time to time and respond to questions that may not be related to day-to-day operation. I have dealt with such issues as capital investment plans, major maintenance spending, vendor selection, customer issues, and a whole host of other topics that will also come up that we need to be open about during discussions with team members. These topics may not be day-to-day issues but can still be relevant issues that owners will want information on from time to time. Be sure you allow for time to have these type discussions. Weekly lunch meetings, monthly plant-wide meetings, and "management by walking around" (MBWA) discussions are also all great forums for such discussions. You may think it is a burden to have these talks with team members, but remember you are creating an ownership culture. And those owners need access to information.

After establishing that new identity and providing access to information, proceed with the other Is to creating an ownership culture. These can be implemented in any order and can also be done simultaneously. Do what works best for your organization. I would suggest implementing ones that are easier for your organization to facilitate momentum building in this transformation process. Organizations will be at different places in the engagement spectrum and find different Is easier or more challenging to implement than someone else would consider it. Regardless of the progression selected, the key is to be consistent with the approach and focus. Everything matters when you are making a major culture change such as the one described here. You can't put it on hold for another major project or challenge that may arise during implementation. You hold firm to this culture change through those projects or challenges to get the most impactful leadership opportunity. Too many leaders have a short-term, win-now focus. We are all really in this game of business or service for the long-term. While we all want to be successful now, don't make short-term decisions that hinder long-term sustained success. Think long term, but live in the present.

Key learnings:

1. Engagement is really all about leadership
2. The benefits of a culture change to ownership touch every facet of the organization
3. Changing culture can be a grind, but over time, it can make a big difference
4. Think long term, but live in the present.

CHAPTER 13

THE LEADER'S CHALLENGE

As I embarked on the mission to write this book, I obviously reflected on my past thirty-plus years leading others. Those leadership opportunities came in my vocation, my church commitments, and various opportunities in the communities that we lived. I recall some great learning experiences and successes, some of which were shared in the prior chapters. I also can't help but think back and wonder how many opportunities that I may have missed. I wonder how many lives that I could have impacted for the better if I had just known more and been more inclined to take more decisive action sooner.

With the regrets and mistakes along the way, there were also so many good memories and stories to tell. I recall so many individuals that partnered with me in this effort to create a better work environment that advanced their careers and had so much influence in their own endeavors. I look back on so many leaders today that started in seemingly small leadership roles that have risen to significantly expanded roles of influence. It is very fulfilling for me to see so many individuals having so much impact in so many places today using the concepts that we developed together over time.

As we consider our role as leaders, the progression for impacting others will generally follow the process noted below. As you read through this progression, give consideration to your current condition related to each of these items to ensure you are equipped to effectively move forward with your culture-changing initiative.

1. Internal genuine care and concern for those we lead.

    This care and concern does not make us a soft, passive leader, but rather drives us to seek the best for our followers. There will be tough discussions and accountability while seeking the best for the followers at times. All these leadership actions though come from a genuine care and concern. For many, a focus on engagement was seen as a distraction from the "real focus" of managing the business. I don't know about you, but I want to go beyond just managing the business and actually lead the business to achieve more, both reaching our goals and fulfilling our purpose. A very key part of that purpose is having a positive impact on the people I lead. Are they really better off in life with my being their leader? That's a big question that I want to be able to answer with a resounding yes!

2. Awareness of the problem and opportunity

    We can all get caught up in the business of the job, the day, and life in general. I have been there far too many times. It took years for me to "slow the game down" and become more aware of the needs around me. I wonder how many opportunities I missed over the years being caught up in the busyness of work. Some of this busyness was likely just a reflection of pride on my part. I always wanted to be timely with responses to corporate and to get as many things done on my list as possible. There were too many instances that I was focused on getting good things done and not being aware of the needs around me. Accomplishments are great, but not at the expense of awareness. I was often focused on what I thought to be the urgent matters of the moment and missed the most important opportunities around me. Those opportunities were often people related. We need to slow down and be more aware of the people around us, particularly those we are leading.

3. Equipped to act on the opportunity.

    It is one thing to have that genuine care and be aware of an opportunity but quite another to be in a position to act on it. I recall learning this fact early on in my high school years in athletics. I had a genuine desire and care to perform at a high level, was very aware of the challenges that I faced, and was sensitive to the opportunities around me. However, I can recall several times early on that I was in a game and just felt overmatched or underprepared. At that moment, I just wished I could go back and work harder to prepare myself for that moment. It's no different here in this discussion of leadership. While we first need that genuine care and concern for those we lead along with an awareness of the opportunities around us, we need to be equipped for action too! We need to invest the time to ensure we are technically equipped for our role, mentally equipped to sustain the challenges, and physically equipped to exhibit the stamina needed at times. In addition, we need to strengthen our communication skills and continue to be an active learner as a leader. We need to commit to reading, listening, and being mentored by others to fully develop as a leader. Leadership can be learned and developed. While some may have a natural personality trait toward leadership, leading others is still a choice and a commitment. I don't know that I was born with that natural instinct, but a strong care and concern for others drove me to see development opportunities in that direction. Invest the time, and be ready when the opportunities arise. Be prepared to be the leader your followers deserve.

4. Be the leader and take action.

    The core internal care have been established. The awareness of challenges and opportunities are in place, and you are equipped to lead well. It's now time to take action and be the leader that your followers need you to be. It's now time to provide that vision, make sacrifices for your followers, and lead them well. Leaders take action, remove obstacles, communicate strategy, and work with the team to execute at a high level. Leaders stay engaged, listen to people, and adapt as needed. Leadership is a selfless pursuit that is focused outward and always seeking the long-term best outcome for the team members. Leaders are effective when they build credibility, communicate at a high level, and commit themselves to establishing a culture based on valuing and caring for one another.

While leaders may get discouraged from time to time and face major opposition along the way, they stay the course because the ultimate purpose is the key. The purpose is not the comfort and perks of being the leader, but rather the long-term well-being of the followers. When the focus is on others, tough times are just obstacles in the way. We may have to adapt and make revisions, but we don't stop pressing forward in leadership. If we are going to create a culture of ownership in the workplace, it will take consistent work every day to drive that transformation process to completion. In reality, I don't know that we are ever really done, but rather we continually strive to better our work environment for those we lead each day.

If you have made it this far in the book, you are obviously serious about leading well and creating a different culture in your organization. You are obviously serious about real engagement! It's now time to get started. There are key learnings at the end of many of the chapters, and hopefully you had many more identified on your own. Take those key learnings, map out your plan, and get started toward moving your organization toward a culture of ownership. Challenge yourself to do more than make a living. Go make a difference. There are many people out making a living but very few actually making a difference. Create a better workplace for your people and leave a legacy. Do something that you will look back on one day and realize that it was worth the effort. It won't be easy. Leadership is tough, but I want to make sure it's worth it for you. Ultimately, I want to help you be a leader worthy of following!

ABOUT THE AUTHOR

Doug Strickel has over thirty years' experience leading people with Ernst & Young and International Paper Company. He has provided direct leadership to manufacturing facilities, as well as served as a regional general manager over a number of facilities during his tenure with International Paper. Doug is a certified corporate leadership trainer and has been a frequent speaker, writer, and trainer on leadership skills. Now retired from International Paper, Doug has taken this passion for leadership and started Strickel Leadership Development LLC. He provides leadership training sessions, speaking services, and various other support services to organizations of all types. All of these services are aimed at helping others lead more effectively. He frequently posts leadership articles on LinkedIn and shares a monthly leadership blog posting on followerdrivenleadership.com. You can find more information about Doug at dougstrickel.com.